James Cook and Samuel Marsden

Their legacy lives on

James Cook

Samuel Marsden

Cover design by Peysoft Publishing
Second edition - 2019

Printed by Lulu.com

ISBN: 978-0-9941309-6-9

Kindle: TBA

eBook: 978-1-365-40828-1

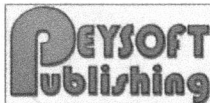

Paeroa
2019

Contents

Time Line

1000 (approx.) – Maori settled the Bay of Islands

1642 – Abel Jans Tasman named New Zealand 'Staten Landt'

1769 – James Cook circumnavigated New Zealand (1st of 3 voyages)

1772 – Marc Joseph Marion du Fresne killed and eaten

1804 – Te Pahi meets Samuel Marsden at Port Jackson, Australia

1814 – Samuel Marsden conducts first Christian service at Rangihoua

1827 – The Kings and Shepherds are the only missionaries at Rangihoua.

1828 – Hongi Hika dies of wounds received in battle.

1830 – Samuel Marsden encourages the 4th Mission settlement at Waimate.

1832 – Rangihou mission closes – moved to Te Puna, two kilometres west.

1834 – James Busby, British Govt Representative, takes up Residence at Waitangi

1836 – Stone Store (oldest in NZ) commences trade. Kemp house built.

1837 – Samuel Marsden's 7th Visit.

1838 – Samuel Marsden dies in Sydney

1839 – Mangungu Mission, Hokianga Harbour, built.

1840 – Treaty of Waitangi

1842 – French built 'Pompellier Mission & Printery' at Russell

Glossary

Aroha – love; caring for others

Hangi – food cooked in an earth oven; the actual earth oven

Hapu – tendency to violence and revenge / extended family

Hongi – to press noses

Iwi – tribe

Koha – gift

Makutu – to lay a curse

Marae – meeting place

Pakeha – person of fair skin

Tapu – Sacred, forbidden

Te Rongopai o Ihu Karaiti - the Gospel of Jesus Christ
Te Kaiwhakaora mō te iwi katoa - the Saviour for all people
Utu – to seek redress
Whakanoa – the act of releasing from tapu / forbidden
Whakapapa – genealogy
Whanau – family
Whare – house or building

Preface

As a tenth generation South African and a new immigrant to New Zealand, I found James Cook and Samuel Marsden to be two of the most interesting personalities involved in the colonial civilisation of the Maori.

Portuguese and Spanish ships began crossing the Pacific Ocean in the 1500s, but it was probably not until 1642 that a European sighted New Zealand. In that year the Dutch explorer Abel Tasman sailed in search of a vast southern continent, which many Europeans thought might exist in the South Pacific. Dutch merchants hoped this land would offer new opportunities for trade. Tasman discovered New Zealand on 13 December 1642, but after a bloody encounter with Māori in Golden Bay, he left without going ashore, or so it is claimed.

The first European to set eyes on the country was frightened off in December 1642 when confronted by cannibalism in Golden Bay, which he named Murderers' Bay. He named New Zealand 'Staten Landt'

Shortly afterwards, a Dutch map maker gave the name Nieuw Zeeland to the land Tasman had discovered.

Frenchman Jean François Marie de Surville had left India on the *St Jean Baptiste* in March 1769 to explore the South Pacific and seek trade. He sailed via Malacca and the Solomon Islands and reached the western coast of New Zealand – thus being the first European to see NZ after Tasman – in December 1769. He lost a lot of his crew to scurvy and just missed James Cook while rounding North Island. de Surville anchored in Doubtless Bay for two weeks and while there lost three anchors during a December storm.

James Cook circumnavigated New Zealand three times, between 1769 and 1779. A most remarkable man who mapped the two islands accurately with a sextant and plotting the country accurately at Mercury Bay. Whereas his first encounter with the warlike Maori also led to bloodshed, his relations with another iwi were more favourable. A large section of this book is devoted to Cook's explorations.

Not far behind Cook and de Surville came another Frenchman, Marc Joseph Marion du Fresne, who had served on French India Company ships. He undertook to return a Tahitian, brought by Bougainville to Paris, to his home island. He was also to seek out the legendary southern continent. His ships the *Marquis de Castries* and *Mascarin* sailed from Mauritius in October 1771, called at Cape Town, then headed east. After landfall at New Zealand's Cape Egmont, he sailed around the top of the North Island.

A long stay in the Bay of Islands was necessary to repair his ships, which had been damaged by a collision in the Indian Ocean. The ships were anchored in the bay from 4 May to 12 July 1772. Many of the initial encounters between Māori and the French were friendly. The expedition left an extensive record of Māori life.

However, the situation in the Bay of Islands was volatile, as Ngāpuhi tribal groups were gradually displacing the earlier Ngāti Pou inhabitants. The French presence destabilised the situation further, and misunderstandings were rife. In mid-June, Marion du Fresne and 24 others were killed by Māori. What sealed his fate seems to have been an inadvertent violation by the French of a sacred restriction ("Tapu") placed by Māori on a particular bay. The French took savage revenge for their captain's death before returning to Mauritius via the Philippines.

Samuel Marsden, a missionary, also made his mark with establishing the Christian faith and bringing education to Maori. Although based in Australia, he befriended influential Maoris, establishing several mission stations during his eight visits to the country. The first being in 1814 and the last in 1837, a year before he died in Sydney. Marsden is perhaps best known for holding the first Christian church service in New Zealand over two hundred years ago on Christmas day 1814, with his scripture reading from Luke's Gospel 2.10 - *'Behold! I bring you glad tidings of great joy'*.

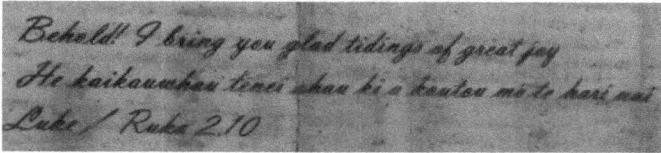

The inscription appears at the start of the Marsden Cross Walk at Oihi

Abel Tasman

Dutchman Abel Tasman was the first European to sight New Zealand on the 13th December 1642.

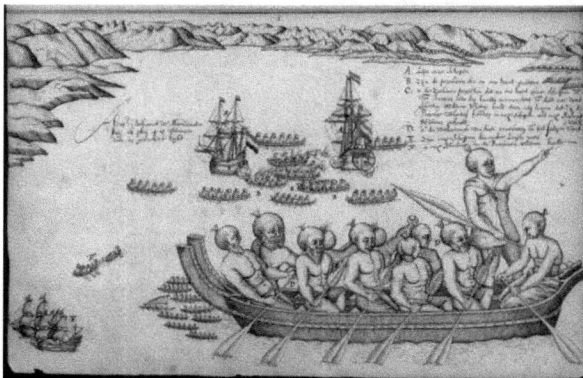

Murderer's Bay (now Golden Bay) drawing by Abel Tasmans' artist Isaack Gilsemans. Two wakas lashed together, carrying twelve Maoris

James Cook

James Cook's ship the *Endeavour* was a relatively small vessel of 368 tons, just 32 metres long and 7.6 metres broad. It departed from Plymouth on 26 August 1768 with 94 men, entering the Pacific around Cape Horn. After almost four months in Tahiti, from mid-April to mid-August, the *Endeavour* sailed south into uncharted waters.

James Cook

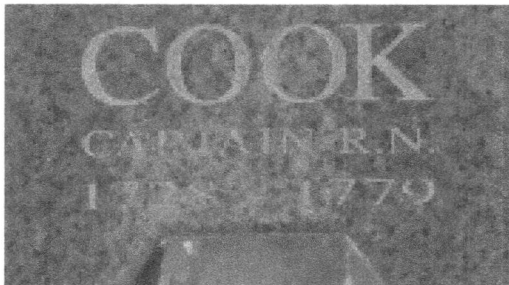

Sailing across uncharted seas in October 1769, James Cook offered a reward of rum to the man who first sighted land, and promised that 'that part of the coast of the said land should be named after him'.

On 6 October 1769 cabin boy Nicholas Young sighted land.

The surgeon's boy had probably come aboard the ship in the retinue of the botanist, Joseph Banks. It is not recorded if Young Nick was given the rum, but the headland below the high hills which he first saw from the masthead was named Young Nicks Head after him. He was certainly sharp-eyed because he was also the first to see Land's End when the *Endeavour* returned to England in 1771.

The Endeavour

The ship's surgeon's boy Nicholas Young who was on the masthead of the Endeavour, sighted land on the 6th October 1769 – shouting "Land!"

Two days later the Endeavour sailed into Tuurangi-nui Bay at the entrance to the Gisborne River. Cook named the peninsular Young Nick's Head.

Cook realised the coast was occupied when he noticed smoke along the coastline. He went ashore, with a group of sailors in two small boats, in search of fresh water and refreshments and also to establish friendly relations with the inhabitants. Four sailors who were left to guard the boats were suddenly surprised by the appearance of four warlike Maori brandishing weapons. When one Maori lilted a lance to hurl at the boat, he was shot and killed by the coxswain. Cook's party returned to the Endeavour but came ashore the next day with Tupaia who could communicate with the Maori in their language, which was similar to his Pacific Island language. Despite gifts being presented, the Maori remained hostile. When one Maori seized a cutlass, he was shot. The following day two canoes approached the *Endeavour* and attacked one of *Endeavours* small boats. The occupants returned fire, killing or wounding a further three or four Maori.

James Cook was upset by the killings and decided to leave the area. He named the area Poverty Bay. He sailed south, without taking any refreshments aboard.

On the 15th October, a large canoe with about 20 Maori came alongside the Endeavour where, with the help of linguist Tupaia, "traded some stinking fish'. Cook wished to trade a piece of red cloth in exchange for a dog skin cloak. But after inspecting the offering, as Tupaia's servant Tayeto was about to take possession of the traded fish, Tupaia was captured and the Maori made off at great speed. Cook's men fired on the canoe, killing one Maori. Tayeto leaped overboard and was picked up by the Endeavour. Cook named the area Kidnapper's Bay.

Unfortunate skirmishes on that day and the next resulted in the deaths of several Māori. The incidents appear, like Tasman's bloody experience at Murderers' Bay (Golden Bay) in 1642, to have been in part the result of Māori efforts to deal with strange newcomers in a traditional way. After the encounters, Cook sailed first south to Cape Turnagain, then north, pausing at Tolaga Bay and Anaura Bay before rounding East Cape to Mercury Bay. After a week in the Bay of Islands, he turned the top of the North Island in a storm and sailed down its west coast.

From there the Endeavour continued to Cape Turnagain, turning around to the East Cape and the Bay of Plenty. On 3rd November, suitable anchorage was found at Mercury Bay – so named as ten days were spent there observing the transit of Mercury. Before leaving Mercury Bay, the date and the ship's name Endeavour were carved into a tree, and Cook took formal possession of this area.

Cooks Landing at Mercury Bay – a dreary, overcast day when Rina and I visited the exact spot

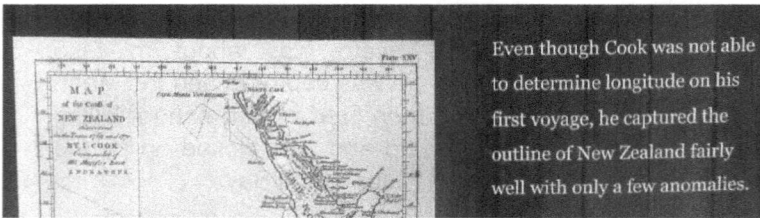

Even though Cook was not able to determine longitude on his first voyage, he captured the outline of New Zealand fairly well with only a few anomalies.

Cook's chart of the Coromandel outline was remarkably accurate, considering the track he sailed around it.

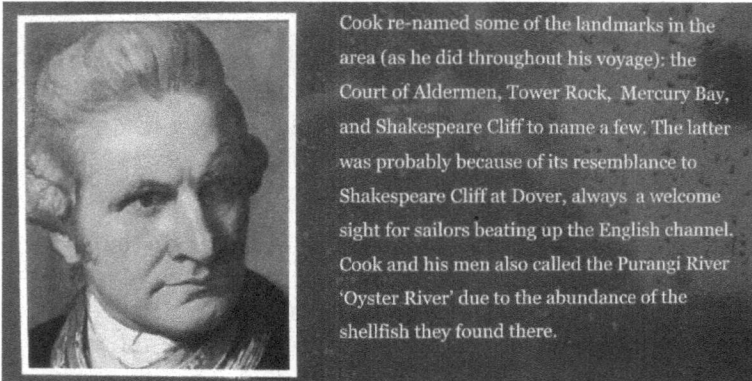

Cook re-named some of the landmarks in the area (as he did throughout his voyage): the Court of Aldermen, Tower Rock, Mercury Bay, and Shakespeare Cliff to name a few. The latter was probably because of its resemblance to Shakespeare Cliff at Dover, always a welcome sight for sailors beating up the English channel. Cook and his men also called the Purangi River 'Oyster River' due to the abundance of the shellfish they found there.

Cook re-named some of the landmarks in the area (as he did throughout his voyage): The Court of Alderman, Tower Rock, Mercury Bay, and Shakespeare Cliff to name a few. He also called the Purangi River 'Oyster River' due to the abundance of the shellfish they found there.

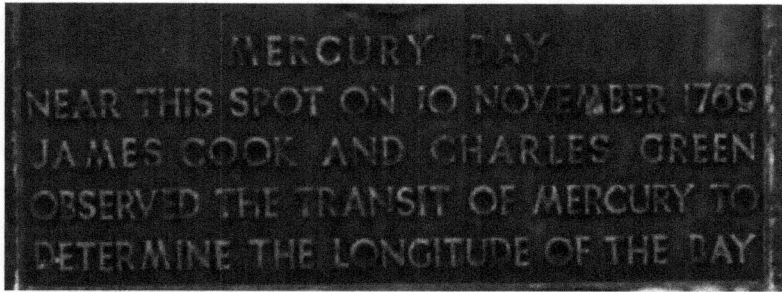

Inscription reads "Mercury Bay: Near this spot-on 10 November 1769 James Cook and Charles Green observed the transit of Mercury to determine the longitude of the Bay.

Five days later the *Endeavour* passed around Cape Colville and into the Hauraki Gulf, dropping the anchor about halfway along the Coromandel Coast.

Cook was the first European explorer to go by boat up the Waihau river from current Thames to nearby Netherton, north-west of Paeroa. Rina my wife and I visited this historical spot several times – with our campervan Titanic and with Rina's sister, Gerta Bezuidenhout.

An anchor, donated by the Royal New Zealand Navy has been mounted on the bend of the river to commemorate the event. His actual landing spot is a short distance down river from 'Cooks Landing."

Cooks Landing – Netherton / Paeroa, Hauraki Plains

Sisters Gerta Bezuidenhout and Rina Geldenhuys

Sailing further north, the *Endeavour* arrived at the Bay of Islands.

While navigating around the northern tip of New Zealand on 13th December, the *Endeavour* ran into strong gales off Cape Marie van Diemen, forcing the ship off course. About nine miles offshore and in daylight hours, the *Endeavour* passed by the French ship St. Jean-Baptiste, under the command of Jean-François-Marie de Surville, struggling to remain on course but in the opposite direction.

Cooks actual landing – to carve his name and date on a tree

The Cook Party landing site 1.3km along Captain Cook road.
The plinth in December 2019

Original 'anchor' memorial; Sarjant's corner, 1975

*Plinth with anchor (subsequently stolen) and Karen Geldenhuys
pointing to the metal inscription of Cook's landing (Nov 1769)*

Hall's (28m)	Cook's (c. 45m)	Largest existing	Kauri
142 years old	c. 280 years old	kahikatea (Pirongia - 66.5m)	(Tane Mahuta 51m)

The 2000-year old Tane Mahuta Kauri tree is well known by most New Zealanders. This image compares the size and ages of 'Cook's Tree which was subsequently felled. The actual spot is no longer recognizable.

The next image is the Kenney family photo of Cook's tree when it was felled. This was the start of the Coromandel becoming the favoured area to harvest trees for ships masts.

Ohinemuri Regional History Journal 12, October 1969

About 1900, Captain Cook's Tree, Kahikatea, Netherton (hollow when felled). Courtenay, Alic and Daisy Kenny, (Mrs Bray). Photo by courtesy Charlie Murdock.

Kenny family photo reputed to be Cook's kahikatea stump and section of trunk (Photo also held by Paeroa Museum)

Dave Wilton in The Treasury Journal examines the travels and landmarks of James Cook's ship HMS Endeavour in the Firth of Thames - Waihou River area during November 1769. There are three main sites of interest related to Cook's visit to the Firth of Thames area: the Endeavour's anchorage in the Firth, the pa site visited when Cook and a small party voyaged by two ship's boats up the Waihou, and the place where they went ashore to measure a large kahikatea, which was probably also the limit of their journey up the river.

Heading north up the coast to the Bay of Islands. Cook spent a week in this bay, which was to become the first site of permanent European settlement.

The "St Jean Baptise" was a French Indian ship on a trading mission. Its Commander was looking for a bay in which to anchor to take on fresh water and fruit for his scurvy ridden crew. The "St Jean-Baptiste" knew nothing of Captain James Cook and the Endeavour, just a short distance away. Incredibly, neither the British nor the French sighted each other.

On 17th December the St Jean-Baptiste laid anchor at Doubtless Bay, in the North Island. The Bay had been given this name by Captain Cook, as on sighting it for the first time from afar, he is reported to have said "this is doubtless a bay".

In the beginning of January 1770, as the Endeavour was sailing down the western coast, Mount Taranaki was sighted. Cook named it Mount Egmont, after the First Lord of the Admiralty.

On the 14th January, the Endeavour arrived at "a very broad and deep bay or inlet". The ship was in the South Island of New Zealand, and in this inlet a perfect anchorage was found at Ship Cove. Cook named the inlet Queen Charlotte's Sound, and took formal possession of this area. Friendly relations were established with the Māori, and trade for fish and fresh vegetables commenced.

The anchorage in Ship Cove, Queen Charlotte Sound, was to be a base on all three voyages, but was pivotal in the second. Cook certainly had a firm attachment to the place, providing as it did a safe anchorage, save for the occasional williwaw, bountiful food and refreshment, plentiful timber for spars and a suitable beach on which to haul up the ship. After tense confrontations with the Maori people of the North Island, he also seemed more trustful and relaxed in his dealings with the local tribes.

On 6th February, the *Endeavour* made for Cook Strait, while surveying the coastline of the South Island. By 13th March the most southern point of the South Island was rounded, and the *Endeavour* commenced coasting up along the west coast. A bay which was passed as night fell was given the name Dusky Bay.

The Endeavour left New Zealand on 31st March 1770, after having spent two days in Admiralty Bay refitting the ship. Cook had just chartered 2 400 miles of New Zealand coastline, in under 6 months.

Cook was to return to New Zealand on two further occasions, once in 1773 in command of the *Resolution*, accompanied by Tobias Furneaux in command of The *Adventure*, and again in 1777 in command of The Resolution, and with Charles Clerke in command of The *Discovery*.

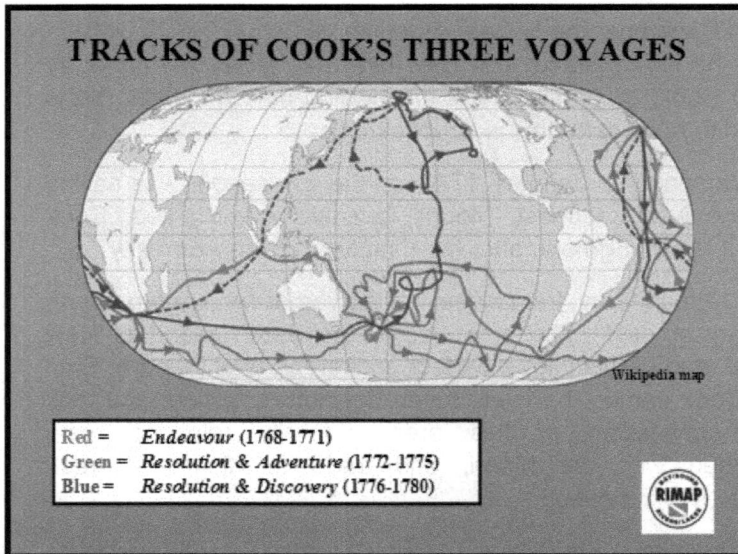

TRACKS OF COOK'S THREE VOYAGES

Wikipedia map

Red = *Endeavour* (1768-1771)
Green = *Resolution & Adventure* (1772-1775)
Blue = *Resolution & Discovery* (1776-1780)

The First voyage was made in the Endeavour 1768 -1771, Second with the Resolution and Adventure 1772 – 1775 and the Third voyage in Resolution and Discovery in 1776 – 1780.

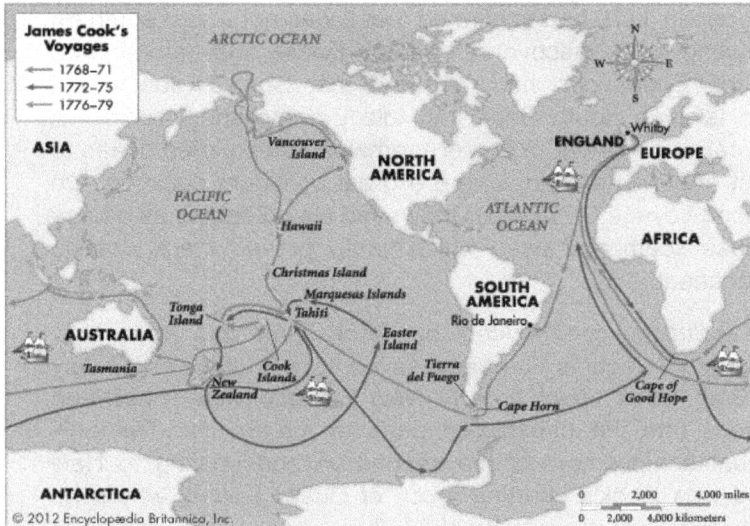

James Cook's Voyages
← 1768–71
← 1772–75
← 1776–79

© 2012 Encyclopædia Britannica, Inc.

A favoured anchorage

On 15 January 1770 Cook brought the *Endeavour* to anchor at Ship Cove in Queen Charlotte's Sound at the top of the South Island. From a high point on Arapawa Island he gained his first view of the narrow strait that now bears his name. Sailing through the strait, he returned to Cape Turnagain, confirming that the North Island was indeed an island. He then sailed south down the east coast of the South Island and round the southern tip of Stewart Island.

Observing the new land sometimes from well out to sea, he made two famous mistakes, charting Banks Peninsula as a probable island and Stewart Island as a probable peninsula. He did not land again until he put into Admiralty Bay, D'Urville Island, on 27 March 1770 for wood and water.

On 1 April 1770 Cook sailed west to discover and chart the eastern coast of Australia. He reached Batavia (Jakarta) on 11 October and returned to England, having circumnavigated the globe, on 13 July 1771.

The second voyage

When Cook made his two subsequent voyages into the Pacific, New Zealand was no longer a place unknown to Europeans. The first voyage in 1770 had confirmed that it was not a vast southern land waiting to be discovered. Joseph Banks, the naturalist on board the *Endeavour*, had recorded that Cook's rounding of Stewart Island's South Cape had totally demolished 'our aerial fabrick called continent'. Yet there remained unexplored ocean to the east of New Zealand, where a great continent could lie. On his second voyage (1772–75) Cook used New Zealand as a base for probes south and east, which finally proved there was no such continent.

The *Resolution*, commanded by Cook, and the *Adventure*, commanded by Tobias Furneaux, sailed from England on 13 July 1772. Both ships spent time in New Zealand waters between excursions into the unexplored parts of the Pacific. The only significant achievement of the second voyage relating to New Zealand was Cook's charting much of Dusky Sound, where he spent six weeks in the autumn of 1773.

Historic tree stumps

Some of the earliest evidence of a European presence in New Zealand is found in the far south-west of the South Island. When James Cook rested up in Dusky Sound in the autumn of 1773 after arduous voyages towards Antarctica, one of the tasks he had his party complete was accurately fixing the geographical position of New Zealand. So that the necessary observations could be made, about an acre (half a hectare) of land on Astronomer Point was cleared of bush. The stumps of trees felled by Cook's men can still be seen beneath the regrown bush.

The third voyage

On his third voyage (1776–79), Cook paid a last visit to New Zealand. He stayed from 12 to 25 February 1777 at 'our old station', Ship Cove in Queen Charlotte's Sound, before sailing into the north Pacific. He was killed in an incident with the islanders at Kealakekua Bay, Hawaii, on 14 February 1779.

James Cook has left a permanent imprint on the consciousness of New Zealanders. Districts, suburbs, schools, hotels, motels, banknotes and consumer products bear his name and likeness. Of more enduring importance, he named more coastal landmarks than any other person, and his own name is attached to two of the country's most significant geographical features, as well as many minor ones.

Cook spent a total of 328 days on the coast of New Zealand during his three voyages, considerably longer than at his other regular stopping place at Tahiti. Daily events were meticulously recorded.

Maori trading potatoes / Kumara for blankets – garments made from woven flax

Early New Zealand nautical maps

Death of James Cook

NEAR THIS SPOT
CAPT. JAMES COOK
MET HIS DEATH
FEBRUARY 14 1779

James Cook's Memorial

Cook Monument

In memory of
the great circumnavigator
Captain James Cook R.N.
who
discovered these Islands
on the 10 th January A.D. 1770
and fell near this spot
on the 14 th of February A.D. 1779

THIS PLAQUE IS TO COMMEMORATE THE MEN WHO BUILT
THE WHITBY SHIPS
'ENDEAVOUR', 'RESOLUTION', 'ADVENTURE', 'DISCOVERY',
USED BY
CAPT. JAMES COOK, R.N., F.R.S.
AND ALSO
THE MEN WHO SAILED WITH HIM
ON THE GREATEST VOYAGES OF EXPLORATION OF ALL TIME
1768 - 1771.   1772 - 1775.   1776 - 1778.

UNVEILED IN THE PRESENCE OF THE
HIGH COMMISSIONERS OF AUSTRALIA AND NEW ZEALAND
ON 26 AUG. 1968
THE BICENTENARY OF HIS FIRST VOYAGE.

"TO STRIVE, TO SEEK, TO FIND AND NOT TO YIELD"

Cook Medallion

Samuel Marsden

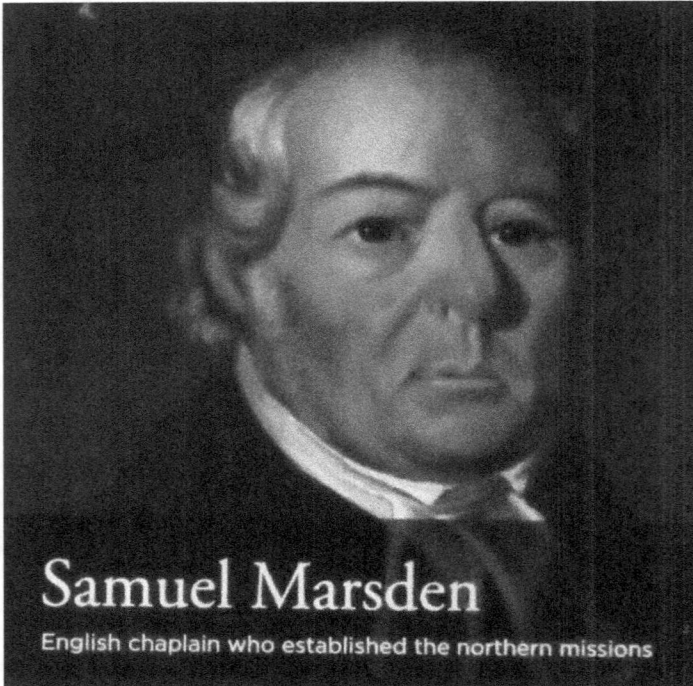

Samuel Marsden
English chaplain who established the northern missions

Samuel Marsden was born on 25 June 1765, at Farsley, Yorkshire, England, the eldest of the seven children of Bathsheba Brown and her husband, Thomas Marsden. He was baptised at Calverley, near Leeds, on 21 July 1765. At the age of 14 or 15 he went to work in his uncle's smithy, and in 1786 was recruited by an Anglican evangelical group, who sent him to Magdalene College, Cambridge, in 1790. Two years later he accepted an appointment as assistant chaplain to the colony of New South Wales. In 1793, he was ordained. He married Elizabeth Fristan at Hull on 21 April 1973.

Of all the early missionaries Samuel Marsden is the best remembered. It was his investigations that first showed that the Maori attacks on ships and their crews were usually the result of previous assaults by the seamen on the natives. Only Henry

Williams, who died and was buried at Pakaraka, comes a close second to Samuel Marsden!

Marsden arrived at Sydney Cove, Australia on 10 March 1794 with his wife and new-born daughter, Ann, the first of their eight children. He took up residence at Parramatta in July, and concerned himself with the welfare of orphan children and female convicts. In October, he took up a 100-acre block, where he quickly put to good use the gardening and farming implements he had brought with him. Late in 1795 he also consented to serve as a magistrate (gaining a reputation for severity) and as superintendent of government affairs.

In the next few years Marsden was very busy, not merely as chaplain and magistrate but as a rising landowner. However, he felt the call to evangelise. He lent his warm support to the infant missions to the South Seas and in 1804 took up the post of local agent for the London Missionary Society's Pacific operations. Marsden's attention gradually turned to the Maori of New Zealand as a promising people for evangelisation. He often accommodated visiting Maori, putting them up in his own house and teaching them, entirely at his own expense. As early as 1805 Te Pahi was a visitor.

The extension of the mission to New Zealand was another matter. In 1800 Marsden had been called on to act as sole chaplain for New South Wales, and it was not until 1807 that he was free to return to London to plead his case before the Church Missionary Society. He then raised a band of lay settlers to prepare the way for ordained missionaries. They were William Hall, a joiner; Thomas Kendall, a schoolmaster; and John King, a ropemaker. It was not until August 1809 that Marsden left England aboard the *Ann* with Hall and King. Ruatara, of Nga Puhi, who was discovered in England in a sick and neglected state, travelled with them and was to spend eight months with Marsden, to whom he taught the rudiments of the Maori language.

The establishment of the New Zealand outpost was further delayed. The missionary societies rejected Marsden's proposal to link Sydney, Tahiti and New Zealand, and, probably in February 1814, he was obliged to buy his own ship, the *Active*, for £1,400, most of which came out of his own pocket. The temporary Colonial Office veto of any further settlement in New Zealand almost proved the last straw. Hall and Kendall (who had come out in 1813) did not reach the Bay of Islands until June 1814; Marsden himself did not arrive until December.

St. John's in Parramatta, 2013.
Photograph by the author

Below left: Mr. Marsden's Church at Parramatta, an engraving of St John's, Parramatta.

J.B. Marsden, Life and Work of Samuel Marsden (Christchurch: Whitcombe & Tombs, 1913), 96

Samuel Marsden's church at Paramatta, Port Jackson, Australia

Time Line

1769 – James Cook circumnavigated New Zealand (1st of 3 voyages)

1772 – Marc Joseph Marion du Fresne killed and eaten

1804 – Te Pahi meets Samuel Marsden at Port Jackson, Australia

1814 – Samuel Marsden conducts first Christian service at Rangihoua

1819 – Samuel Marsden's Second visit

1820 - Marsden's Third visit

1823 – Marsden's Fourth visit

1825 – Samuel Marsden sells the Brig Active for £400

1827 – The Kings and Shepherds are the only missionaries at Rangihoua.

1827 – Samuel Marsden's Fifth visit

1828 – Hongi Hika dies of wounds received in battle.

1830 – Samuel Marsden's Sixth visit

1830 – Samuel Marsden encourages the 4th Mission settlement at Waimate.

1832 – Rangihoua mission closes – moved to Te Puna, two kilometres west.

1834 – James Busby, British Govt Representative, takes up Residence at Waitangi

1836 – Stone Store (oldest in NZ) commences trade. Kemp house built.

1837 – Samuel Marsden's 7th Visit.

1838 – Samuel Marsden dies in Sydney

1839 – Mangungu Mission, Hokianga Harbour, built.

1840 – Treaty of Waitangi

1842 – French built 'Pompelier Mission & Printers' at Russell

The Rev. Samuel Marsden.

Thomas Kendall

First Visit

It was in December, 1814, that Marsden first visited New Zealand.

Marsden was accompanied on his voyage in the brig *Active* by Ngapuhi Ruttara who was his guest at Paramata and several Maori chiefs, returning from Sydney, as well as Thomas Kendall, who had been appointed magistrate to remain in the country. This appointment was made on Marsden's recommendation, with a view to affecting some control over the licentiousness of the whalers and seamen visiting New Zealand.

Three of the chiefs — Dewaterra, Shungee and —were named in Governor Lachlan Macquarie's order of November 9th, 1814, as being invested with somewhat similar powers. Incidentally, Marsden uses a slightly different spelling for their names than that quoted in the official order.

Samuel Marsden meeting Maori chiefs

On his first voyage Marsden arrived at the North Cape on December 16th, 1814, and left Whangaroa for Sydney in the following February. As was always the case with Marsden, he suffered acutely from sea sickness throughout the voyage. A day was spent off North Cape and whilst the chiefs went ashore many canoes brought out an abundance of fish such as Marsden considered "the finest fish I ever saw."

HONGI-HIKA.

The Famous Ngapuhi Warrior.

Whilst at Whangaroa Marsden attempted the difficult task of making peace with the chiefs of the district. In this he was considerably helped by both Duaterra and Shungee (Hongi Hika), two of the chiefs with him. Whangaroa was the scene of the destruction of the *Boyd* and the massacre of the crew in 1809. This happening was investigated by Marsden, who concluded that it was the result of the ill-treatment of the Maoris by the crew in the first place.

(Print, courtesy Alexander Turnbull Library.)
Marsden's Mission-boat escorted by Maori War Canoes in the Bay of Islands.

Historic Rangihoua Bay, Bay of Islands, North of Auckland.

Marsden's decision to sleep with the natives at night was a bold one in view of the fact that at the time he was not yet sure of their intentions and did not know whether they would make peace. There is little doubt that his action must have hastened the reconciliation that took place the next day. In his report Marsden says that he did not sleep much and describes the scene on a beautiful starlit night in these words:-

33

"Around us were numerous spears struck upright in the ground, and groups of natives lying in all directions, like a flock of sheep upon the grass, as there were neither tents nor huts to cover them. I viewed our situation with new sensations and feelings that I cannot express—surrounded by cannibals who had massacred and devoured our countrymen."

On 20 December, at Matauri Bay, Marsden persuaded Ngati Uru and Nga Puhi to make peace. On the 22nd he landed at Rangihoua.

On Christmas Day, 1814, was enacted a scene that had a significance for New Zealand little realized at the time by those taking part in it. Marsden preached the first public service held in the Dominion, taking as his text, "Behold I bring you tidings of great joy." Ruatara translated for him.

Prior to the service a special area, including even a pulpit and a reading desk, had been prepared under the direction of Duaterra. This chief apparently acted as master of ceremonies, being dressed for the occasion in a regimental uniform given him by Governor Macquarie. With his sword in one hand, he used a switch in the other to indicate when those assembled were to stand up and when to sit down. Later he explained the sermon in Maori.

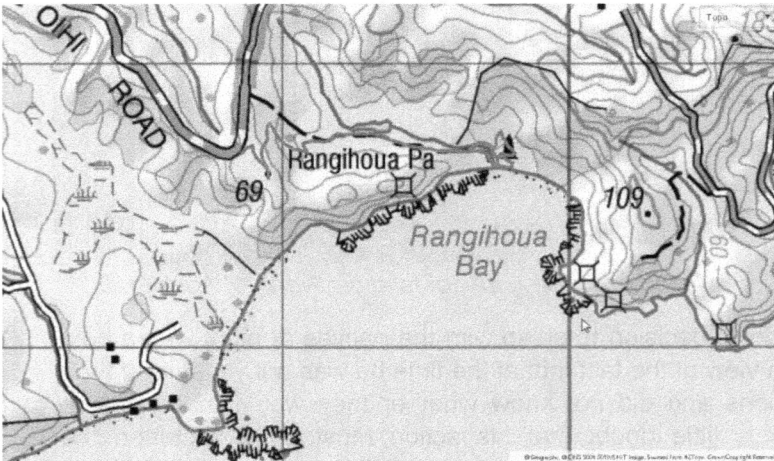

Marsden was mainly desirous of providing for the settlement of those that were to remain behind. On the 26th Marsden set up a charcoal forge to replenish his stock of axes.

Marsden found time to visit several other districts. He penetrated where previously no white man had been. On the 27th he went to Kawakawa to lay in a supply of kahikatea. Early in the new year he perambulated the bounds of his extended parish with Hongi Hika and Ruatara. On 13 January 1815 he went aboard the *Active* with Te Morenga of Tai-a-mai, near Waimate North, another old friend, to prospect the coast as far as the Thames.

His report is full of interesting comments on the customs of the country. He concluded that although all the natives were cannibals it was not due to hunger, but solely as a method of showing "their retaliation and revenge for injuries sustained." He also tried to convince the natives that their punishment of death for theft was too severe. It was their custom to hang thieves. On one occasion Marsden lost three small articles and had it not been for his intervention the culprit would have been killed outright by his chief.

Prior to leaving the country Marsden desired to secure some sort of legal title to the land on which his Missionary settlement was to stand. This area he estimated to comprise some 200 acres and on February 24th, 1815, a formal deed was drawn up and signed. The price paid was twelve axes. It was signed by a chief styled "Ahoodee O Gunna, King of Ranghee Hoo" with a signature that "contains all the lines which are tattooed on the chief's face, according to their singular and curious mode of making thereon drawings and figures."

On 15 February he completed his cargo of flax and timber and on the 24th he left for Sydney. Marsden did not again visit the colony for four years, but he had succeeded in establishing Kendall in residence and arranging for a fairly regular means of communication with Sydney. Considering the short time, he spent in the country he accomplished much.

On the face of it the new venture began well enough. On 20 December, at Matauri Bay, Marsden persuaded Ngati Uru and Nga Puhi to make peace. On the 22nd he landed at Rangihoua, Ruatara's place. On Christmas Day Marsden led off with the Old

Hundredth (Psalm 100) and then preached from Luke 2:10 – 'behold, I bring you good tidings of great joy' – to a large, well-drilled congregation. Ruatara translated for him. On the 26th Marsden set up a charcoal forge to replenish his stock of axes; and on the 27th he went to Kawakawa to lay in a supply of kahikatea. Early in the new year he perambulated the bounds of his extended parish with Hongi Hika and Ruatara. On 13 January 1815 he went aboard the *Active* with Te Morenga of Tai-a-mai, near Waimate North, another old friend, to prospect the coast as far as the Thames. On 15 February, he completed his cargo of flax and timber, and on the 24th, after buying the mission site of some 200 acres at Rangihoua, he cleared for Sydney.

All the same, success was far from assured. In his walks abroad Marsden had seen much want and misery. He had also been made aware of the inveterate jealousy of the hapu, their tendency to violence and revenge, their attachment to tapu and to their own gods. The death of Ruatara soon after Marsden's departure was a serious blow. The evil conduct of the crews of passing ships, the matching of violence with violence, was further cause for concern. In addition, the ever-increasing cost of blankets, clothes and tools for visiting chiefs at Rangihoua and Parramatta, rice and potatoes for Kendall's school, provisions for the mission village at Rangihoua, and the salaries of the New Zealand settlers, was soon a major worry. The *Active* had to be sent whaling to pay her way. There were, before long, personal difficulties with his missionaries. They seemed unable to work amicably together, or to agree on what should be done.

A year or two later things were no better. Marsden's chief ground for complaint at this stage was the private trade in firearms, which he had banned as early as 1815. In February 1819, he was obliged to entreat his settlers once again to desist. They all except Hall agreed to do so, and then promptly yielded to temptation once more. Marsden's own connection with the venture was also in doubt. In New South Wales his material success, and his violent disagreements with the governor, Lachlan Macquarie, and others had caused his missionary ventures to be regarded with suspicion and even contempt. In response to Macquarie's repeated refusal to grant him leave to revisit the Bay of Islands, Marsden took in increasing numbers of Maori at Parramatta and taught them fish-curing, ropemaking, and brickmaking. He also added to his properties so that he could employ all who came in gardening and agriculture, mixed with moral and religious instruction. He plied the settlers at Rangihoua with advice, supplies, and extra hands at his own cost, and kept the *Active* going back and forth, to pick up pork and timber and more visitors.

In mid-1819, with the Church Missionary Society's blessing, Marsden moved to take an even firmer grip on the venture. During his second visit to New Zealand, from 12 August to 9 November 1819, he dismissed two of the settlers and banned once more the traffic in powder and muskets.

On his return to Sydney, Marsden presented to the Church Missionary Society a very lengthy account of his observations. It is characteristic of the age in which he lived that this report opens with much preliminary statement, including even a reference to American Independence. He then proceeds to an historical account of the first missionary contacts with New Zealand, including an account of the visit of various chiefs to Norfolk Island.

Second Visit

Marsden returned five years later on the 12th August 1819 to establish the Kerikeri mission.

The 13,000 Land grand was signed by John Butler and Thomas Kendall on behalf of the CMS / Samuel Marsden and ten Maori Chiefs, headed by Shunghee Heeka (Hongi Hika), Pookay Kohay (Puke Kowai).

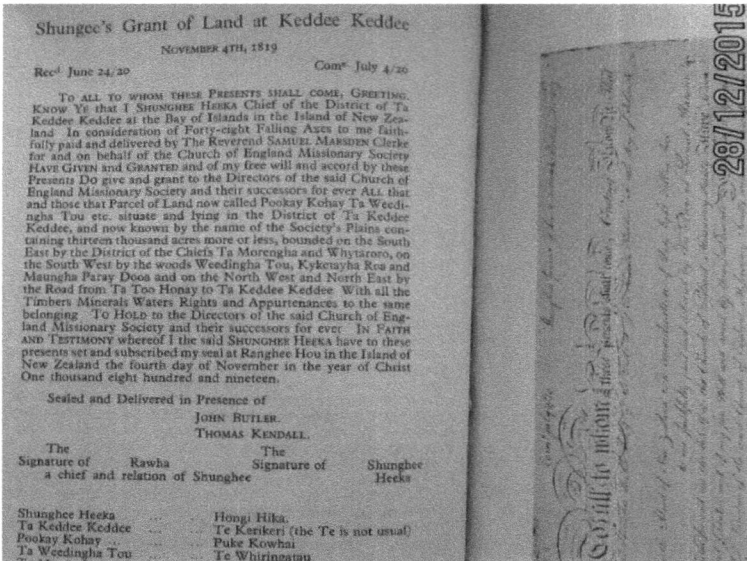

Shungee's Grant of Land at Keddee Keddee

NOVEMBER 4TH, 1819

Rec⁴ June 24/20   Com⁴ July 4/20

To ALL TO WHOM THESE PRESENTS SHALL COME, GREETING. KNOW YE that I SHUNGHEE HEEKA Chief of the District of Ta Keddee Keddee at the Bay of Islands in the Island of New Zealand In consideration of Forty-eight Falling Axes to me faithfully paid and delivered by The Reverend SAMUEL MARSDEN Clerke for and on behalf of the Church of England Missionary Society HAVE GIVEN and GRANTED and of my free will and accord by these Presents Do give and grant to the Directors of the said Church of England Missionary Society and their successors for ever ALL that and those that Parcel of Land now called Pookay Kohay Ta Weedingha Tou etc. situate and lying in the District of Ta Keddee Keddee, and now known by the name of the Society's Plains containing thirteen thousand acres more or less, bounded on the South East by the District of the Chiefs Ta Morengha and Whyniraroa, on the South West by the woods Weedingha Tou, Kykeunyha Rea and Maungha Paray Doos and on the North West and North East by the Road from Ta Too Honay to Ta Keddee Keddee With all the Timbers Minerals Waters Rights and Appurtenances to the same belonging To HOLD to the Directors of the said Church of England Missionary Society and their successors for ever IN FAITH AND TESTIMONY whereof I the said SHUNGHEE HEEKA have to these presents set and subscribed my seal at Ranghee Hou in the Island of New Zealand the fourth day of November in the year of Christ One thousand eight hundred and nineteen.

Sealed and Delivered in Presence of
JOHN BUTLER.
THOMAS KENDALL.

The   The
Signature of   Rawha   Signature of   Shunghee
a chief and relation of Shunghee   Heeka

Shunghee Heeka   ...   Hongi Hika.
Ta Keddee Keddee   ...   Te Kerikeri (the Te is not usual)
Pookay Kohay   ...   Puke Kowhai
Ta Weedingha Tou   ...   Te Whiringatau

Third Visit

In February 1820, at the beginning of his third visit, he remonstrated in vain with Kendall about the latter's impending visit to England with Hongi. In June, 1822 he suspended Kendall for adultery with a Maori woman. He also found himself obliged to report the disobedience of the Reverend John G. Butler, the superintendent of the mission since July 1819.

In the same period, he also set about strengthening the mission. In 1819, he established a new settlement at Kerikeri, and 'bought' from Hongi a 13,000-acre block of land there, which he thought might answer the needs of any poor colonising families the society might send out. In 1820, he stationed James Shepherd with Te Morenga at Tai-a-mai. In August 1823, he opened a further station at Pahia for the Reverend Henry Williams. He also gave what help he could to the infant Wesleyan Methodist mission established at Kaeo, near Whangaroa, in 1823.

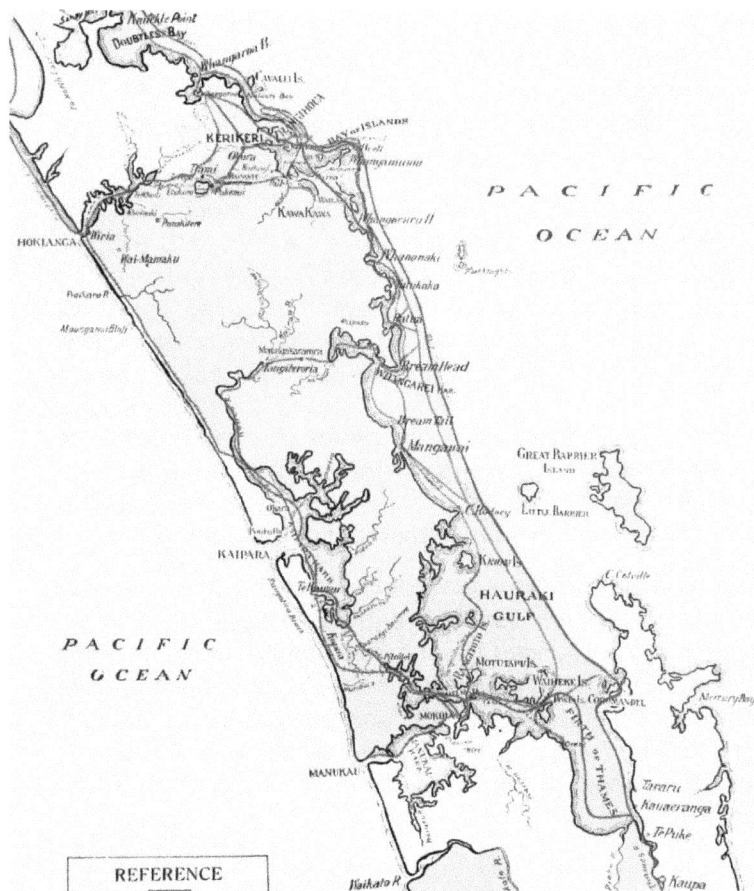

Blue = First journey
Red = Third journey

The objectives of Marsden's visits to New Zealand at this stage were, however, very different in kind. He wanted to see the country and its people, and his remaining journals describe in vivid detail his long journeys, often in rugged, heavily bushed country where no European had ventured. On his third visit, from 27 February to 5 December 1820, he went as far as Tauranga, then back to Kaipara, accompanied by Te Morenga. He also wished to examine at first hand Maori economy, institutions and religious beliefs. Above all, he had come to teach and to preach. Wherever he went he talked, often far into the night, on all manner of subjects – agriculture, commerce, navigation, the principles of government – but especially on the absurdity of tapu, the root cause of all their wars, 'upon the works of Creation, the being and attributes of God, and the institution of the Sabbath Day, and the resurrection of the dead.' He also hoped to press ahead with the translation of the Bible into Maori.

In his later years Marsden was still to suffer much pain and sorrow in the pursuit of what he deemed to be the Lord's will. The setting aside of his claims as archdeacon in 1824 he looked on as of small moment, but he was deeply distressed by W. C. Wentworth's libels in the third edition of *A statistical account of the British settlements in Australasia* (London, 1824), and a reprimand in December by Earl Bathurst, the secretary of state for the colonies, in response to Marsden's charges against the government official H. G. Douglas. He felt he had served his country faithfully and to the best of his ability for 34 years, and at the last had been held up as a promoter of public discord.

The crisis passed, and Marsden's publication in London in 1826 of *an answer to certain calumnies*, and the removal of Douglass from office in 1827, silenced his enemies and produced an effect in his favour in the colony. Even more happily, the new governor, Ralph Darling, encouraged his missionary endeavours, although Marsden's advice to the New Zealand mission was not always accepted. The missionaries, under Henry Williams, often tended to go their own way.

It is recorded *In the Shadows of Moehau* that "When the Reverend Samuel Marsden visited this area in H.M.S. Coromandel in 1820, he climbed Moehau (the highest mountain in the Coromandel Range, rising to 841 metres / 2935ft) and to his amazement saw White Island belching out flames and smoke in an eruption." (The book is in the authors possession).

The Coromandel Story – In Search of the Rainbow it is recorded that *in 1820, Samuel Marsden arrived aboard the HMSS Coromandel which was in the Firth of Thames to collect spars. Having gone ashore to explore the waterways, and flora and fauna, he named this place Coromandel after the ship in which he'd travelled.* (It is believed Marsden was on board the Dromedary)

Like Cook before him, Marsden also navigated the Thames / Waihau river as far as present day Paeroa, then upstream along the Onimuri River to Karangahake Gorge, across the Coromandel / Kaimai mountain Range to Tauranga (mentioned elsewhere).

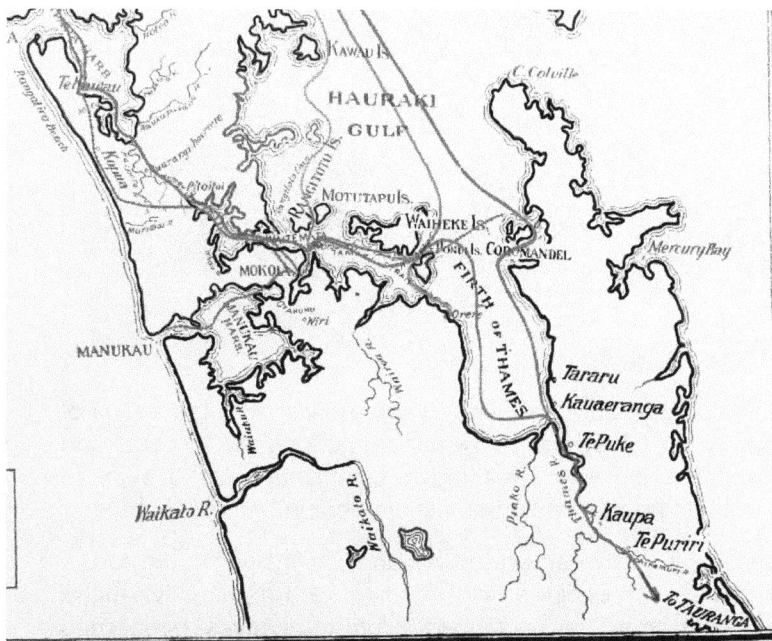

)F NORTHERN NEW ZEALAND
Marsden's journeys of 1814-15 and 1820

Marsden, on board the *HMS Dromedary* in 1820, sailing in company with the tender *Coromandel* - Marsden's Route to 'Towranha' (Tauranga).

The following extract was obtained from the Paeroa Museum. The extract, by CW Vennell, reads as follows:-

'In the following extracts and notes I have endeavoured to establish by an examination of the evidence available, the route followed by the Rev. Samuel Marsden in 1820 when he first visited what he called 'Towrangha'. He was the first white man known to have seen Tauranga Harbour and to have crossed what is now the Waihi district between Paeroa and Katikati".

The letters and Journals of Samuel Marsden, 1765 – 1838: Edited by J.R. Elder 1932.

MARSDEN'S ROUTE TO "TOWRANGHA" IN 1820

By C.W.Vennell

In the following extracts and notes I have endeavoured to establish by an examination of the evidence available, the route followed by the Rev. Samuel Marsden in 1820 when he first visited what he called "Towrangha". He was the first white man known to have seen Tauranga Harbour and to have crossed what is now the Waihi district between Paeroa and Katikati.

The Letters and Journals of Samuel Marsden, 1765—1838 : Edited by J.R.Elder 1932

- - - - - - - - - - - -

P.258. On Friday, July 14th 1820, we were visited (on the Gulf of Thames) by a Chief from Towrangha attended by his son and daughter. The old man was much astonished at the sight of Europeans as he had never seen white people before.

(Prevented by bad weather and floods from making a trip to the Waikato, Marsden decided next day to take a trip to Towrangha by the head of the Thames (River). From the natives he learned that the route led up the Waihou River as far as a pa called Kaupa, which stood near the present site of Paeroa and thence across country. Marsden began his journey upstream on July 17th, partly on foot and partly by canoe. This took three days). Then on:
July20, 1820. After breakfast we set off and in about an hour reached the banks of one of the main branches of the Thames (Waihou) called O Emanonee (Ohinemuri), above Kaupa. About four miles up this river stands a hippah upon a very high stony hill called Tipporari (Te Puriri).

P.258. On Friday, July 14th, 1820, we were visited (on the Gulf of Thames) by a Chief from Towranga attended by his son and daughter. The old man was much astonished at the sight of Europeans as he had never seen white people before.

(Prevented by bad weather and floods from making a trip to the Waikato, Marsden decided next day to take a trip to Towrangha by the head of the Thames (River). From the natives, he learned that the route led up the Waihou River as far as a Pa called Kaupa, which stood near the present site of Paeroa and then across country. Marsden began his journey upstream on July 17th, partly on foot and partly by canoe. This took three days). Then on:

July 20, 1820. After breakfast, we set off and in about an hour reached the banks of one of the main branches of the Thames (Waihou) called O Emanonee (Ohinemuri), above Kaupa (Raupa). About four miles up this river stands a hippah (a pa)) upon a high stony hill called Tipporari (Te Puriri).

We crossed the river O Emanonee at a ford at the foot of the hill. The ford was breast high, and the stream rapid; four New Zealanders carried me over on their shoulders in safety . . . I had 14 natives, including chiefs and their servants with me so that I was under no apprehensions of meeting impediments which, with their assistance I could not overcome.

At this part of the country is very hilly and covered with timber: some of the trees are exceeding lofty and fine. The woods extend to the right and left of the pathway further than the eye can reach. O Emanonee runs through a deep chasm in the mountain (the Karangahake Gorge) at the foot of some very high conical rocks on the right, and we had to ford this river three times, and our path lay through the wood directly across the summit of the hill.

The wood may be about three miles wide at the place we passed through it, but of its length I could form no opinion as I could see no end to it even after I had got upon the high clear land on the opposite side, from which, as the country in the rear of the wood is all open, the hills that encompass Towrangha are clearly to be seen. They appeared to be about 16 miles distant, situated on the skirts of an intervening plain which is pretty level, covered with fern and completely clear of timber.

In this plain, there are several natural springs of water by the foot of the hills which overlook Towrangha, all sending their tributary streams to the O Emanonee --- this river being formed and supplied by the union of these waters. . .

The day was far spent when we reached the plain. We walked on till the sun was nearly set, when we stopped and prepared for the night. The servants who had the provisions to carry (these included a hog – killed and roasted for the journey) were very tired. There were no huts on the plain nor any inhabitants, and we were therefore compelled to take up our lodging in the open air. I was very weary, having had no rest the previous night and having come a long day's journey, so that I felt that rest would be very acceptable even on a heap of fern or on anything else . . .

Friday 21st July. We rose this morning at dawn, and immediately prepared for our journey. I felt much refreshed from the comfortable rest I had enjoyed. We walked for two hours and then sat down, made a fire and cooked our breakfast. The day was favourable tolerably good except where a few small swamps, produced by the springs, intervened. . . When we reached the hills that overlooked Towrangha, which lies about a mile distant below them (actually two miles from Hikurangi summit – 1303 feet – to the foreshore) I sat down on the summit of one of the highest to take a view of the ocean, the islands in sight and the mainland around. The prospect from this height is truly grand . . .

(Te Moreng tells Marsden of his raid on Tauranga early in 1820).

When we had finished this interesting conversation on the hill we walked down to the settlement. Provisions in abundance for our whole party were immediately got ready and we spent the evening very pleasantly.

As far as I could learn no ships had been at Towrangha since Captain Cook was there – (Cook's nearest approach to Tauranga was to anchor off Mayor Island for a night). They are much in want of tools of every kind as they are not visited by any Europeans. Supplies for ships might be got here as they had plenty of potatoes and pork.

Saturday, July 22nd. When we took our leave they (their Maori hosts) accompanied us up the hill with songs and dances. We here met a chief and his wife belonging to Tipporari, the hippah (Pa) I have already mentioned, who accompanied us on our return. We reached before dark the spot on the plain where we had lodged before and remained there all night, having made a screen of brushwood and fern to shelter us from the rain which now began to fall.

Sunday, July 23rd. As soon as the day returned we prepared again for our journey. We reached the hippah about two o'clock.

(After a meal Marsden continued to the Waihou River spending the night at a pa and leaving with the tide early Monday morning, 24th.

Dr. Edward Shortland's Diaries and Journal, 1842 – 44: (MS in Auckland Public Library).

(Dr Shortland, a younger brother of Lieutenant Willoughby Shortland, R.N., was an M.A. of Cambridge. He was appointed private secretary to Governor Hobson in 1941, when he was 29. The following year he was made sub-protector of aborigines and later protector).

Note: In May 1842, the powerful Thames chief Taraia attacked a small number of Ngai-te-rangi in Ongare Pa, near Katikati. The chief Te Whanake was surprised and killed and, according to Dr Shortland his body was with others devoured on the track over which Marsden must have passed 22 years before. This is said to have been the last cannibal feast in New Zealand (vide New Zealand Biography, Vol. II, P.366).

Fourth Visit

The purpose of the Fourth Voyage, in August 1823, was to establish the Paihia mission.

Marsden sailed from Sydney in the *Brampton* on July 22nd, 1823 and reached the Bay of Islands on August 3rd. On September 7^{th,} the *Brampton* sailed from Rangihoua, but struck that day on a sunken reef and was wrecked. No lives were lost, all in the vessel escaping to the island of Moturoa.

Marsden took the Rev Henry Williams, his wife and two children with him, who he settled on the south side of the Bay of Islands, about sixteen miles from Kiddee Kiddee (Kerikeri), twelve miles from Rangheehoo and twelve from Payheea (Paihia).

Marsden also performed the unpleasant task of dismissing Thomas Kendall from CMS service – Kendall had taken a Maori chief's daughter for a wife, which conduct was against CMS behaviour standards.

Marsden achieved much during this visit – he settled and established a new mission, explored the Kawakawa river, dismissed Kendall. He also witnessed Hongi / Shunghee doing battle with a rival chief, Enakkee.

Kendal's Story

Kendall's relationship with the other settlers deteriorated rapidly. He attempted unsuccessfully to assert his leadership, using his influence with Hongi against them. Nevertheless, they all endorsed the letter he wrote on 27 September 1821 which identified their difficulties and argued their need to conciliate with the Maori 'in every possible way'. He defended the gun trade, in which he himself had begun to deal. He told the CMS that the settlers could not dictate to the Maori what articles 'they must receive in payment for their property & services. They dictate to us! ...It is evident that ambition and self-interest are amongst the principal causes of our security amongst them.' This provocative letter was the immediate cause of his dismissal by the CMS in August 1822.

His outspokenness was compounded by the rumours spreading, late in 1821, about his affair with Tungaroa, daughter of Rakau, the old tohunga of Rangihoua. She had been taught by Kendall at the school, and was a servant in his household. Once the news broke he fled with her to Kaihiki, a village on the Te Puna inlet, near to the mission station, but ended the relationship in April 1822. He later tried to explain to a ship's captain that he had lived with her 'to obtain accurate information as to their religious opinions and tenets, which he would in no other way have obtained'; sophisticated perhaps, but not without some truth. Rakau must have been one of Kendall's major informants.

In a series of letters written between 1822 and 1824, mostly to the CMS, Kendall attempted to describe Maori cosmological thought. He sent seven letters, together with three shipments of carvings (now lost), and a drawing of the entrance to a carved storehouse, which is the earliest known illustration of such a structure. This portrayed Nukutawhiti, the canoe ancestor of Nga Puhi. Kendall also published a letter under the pseudonym 'Solicitus' in the Sydney Gazette on 8 January 1831.

Kendall argued that the carvings, attached to war canoes, storehouses and elsewhere, were images depicting three 'states' of existence. The first state he described as undistinguished, formless matter before life; the second was life in this world; and the third, life after death. The drawing of Nukutawhiti is of the ancestor in the first state of existence. But Kendall's descriptions are not clear. They were also distorted by his reading – under the illusion that the Maori were descendants of the Egyptians – of late eighteenth century accounts of Egyptian religious beliefs, particularly from his 1797 edition of the Encyclopaedia Britannica. It is probable, however, that he came closer to understanding the symbolic content of the carvings than anyone ever would again.

Marsden, having learned of Kendall's adultery, came to New Zealand in August 1823 to dismiss him. Kendall agreed to leave, but when the *Brampton,* on which the Kendalls had embarked, was wrecked on a shoal in the Bay he changed his mind.

Marsden's brief visits to the Bay of Islands were packed with action. On his fifth visit, in April 1827 aboard the *Rainbow*, he pointed out to various chiefs their crimes in robbing the Wesleyans at Whangaroa. On 14th November Marsden again left the Bay of Islands in the *Dragon*, which, after a stormy voyage, reached Port Jackson on the 30th.

Fifth Visit

The fifth voyage in 1827 was the briefest of visits, a mere five days, after hearing of the conflict at Whangaroa harbour, between Hongi Hika and Ngati Pou.

The Mission Station at Kerikeri in 1824.

From the *Atlas* of the
Histoire du Voyage de la Coquille
(Paris, 1826).

The *Coquille*, commanded by Captain L. I. Duperrey, reached the Bay of Islands on April 4th, 1824, and remained there for a fortnight. Renamed the *Astrolabe* in memory of the lost navigator La Pérouse, and commanded by Captain Dumont d'Urville, who had served as a lieutenant under Duperrey, the vessel again visited New Zealand in 1826-7, and in 1840. On April 26th of that year she entered the Bay of Islands and remained there for a week during the excitement caused by the arrival of Governor Hobson and the signing of the Treaty of Waitangi.

While the *Coquille* lay in the Bay of Islands in 1824, Dumont d'Urville remarks, " the most amiable relations were maintained between the French and the natives, and several officers made an interesting visit to Kidi-Kidi (Kerikeri), the principal station of the English missionaries at this place."—Dumont d'Urville, *Voyage de la corvette l'Astrolabe* (Paris, 1831), Vol. I, p. 7, and Vol. III, p. 672.

The Kerikeri Mission Station in 1824

ÉTABLISSEMENT DES MISSIONAIRES ANGLAIS À KIDIKIDI (NOUVELLE ZÉLANDE)

Kidikidi alias Kerikeri

An early painting – illustrating Maori dress

The Kerikeri Mission station in 2016

Sixth Visit

On his sixth visit, with his daughter Mary, from March to May 1830, Marsden played a vital part in restoring peace between the rival armies in the bloody Girls' War **at Kororareka (Russell)**. Another significant move was to set up a farm at Waimate North, to render the settlers less dependent on uncertain and expensive supplies from New South Wales and to set an example of peaceful, constructive industry.

Te Waimate Mission was established 1831 to free the New Zealand mission from dependence on the welfare of the CMS.

He threw himself into the work of teaching the small groups of anxious young inquirers who visited him in the evenings, and preaching in Maori to the crowds who gathered round him wherever he went.

Portrait of Repa, antagonist of Hone
Heke, 1847

Seventh Voyage

Marsden never really retired, although in his later years he began to show signs of wear and tear. In October 1835 Elizabeth Marsden died. She had been disabled since 1811. The following December Marsden himself was taken ill. He recovered, but still refused to rest. In February 1837, with his daughter Martha, he undertook yet another voyage to New Zealand, at his own expense. This visitation assumed the proportions of a triumphal procession. At Hokianga hundreds came to pay their respects to the grand old man. On his arrival at Waimate North, where he was borne on a litter through the bush, he was greeted with reverence. On 1 April, he visited Kaitaia where Maori came in party after party. For all his physical weakness, he nonetheless threw himself into the ordinary business of the mission. He not only spent endless hours at committee meetings on all manner of subjects, but ventured many times with Henry Williams into the rival grog-drenched, convict-infested pa, in a vain effort to negotiate an enduring peace between Pomare II and Titore. More happily, he visited most of the mission stations within 100 miles of Waimate North, to teach and preach to their scattered parishioners and to lend the weight of his name to the rapid spread of the arts of reading and writing, the diffusion of peace and order and of the Gospels.

His final departure was on 2 June 1837 aboard the *Rattlesnake*, via the Thames and Cloudy Bay. On his arrival at Sydney he spoke of returning to New Zealand perhaps once a year. He became progressively feebler, however, and on 12 May 1838, on a visit to Windsor, he breathed his last. He was buried in the churchyard of St John's Church, Parramatta.

Marsden's last visit was made on the 23rd February 1837, crossing the treacherous bar of the Hokianga harbour – sailing inland to the Wesleyan Missionary Station where Marsden stayed, with his Martha his youngest daughter, for thirteen days, before travelling inland for seventy miles to Waimate. He was kindly received by the Reverend William Williams and his colleagues and was pleased to note the progress since his last visit.

Marsden then proceeded to the Kerikeri mission, arriving there on the 30th May where he boarded the *Rattlesnake* captained by Hobson and set sail for their Thames Station, arriving there on the 6th June 1837. The main purpose of this visit, during his advancing age, and following the death of his wife, was to confront the issue of misconduct of the Rev William Yate. This weighed heavily on Marsden and took its toll on his failing health in his advancing years. On enquiring, Marsden found the charges against Yale as correct and persuaded Yale to depart the Island within three days. Yale agreed to do so, but shortly thereafter changed his mind; he left three months later notice that his brother had died in the UK.

They sailed around North Island, through the Cook Strait, arriving back in Sydney on the 27th July 1937, having travelled by land and water upwards of 2,000 miles.

Samuel Marsden died at Windsor, New South Wales, on May 12th, 1838, having nearly finished his seventy-third year. He served the CMS for some forty-five years, and was buried in the churchyard of his church at Parramatta.

The Marsden Cross

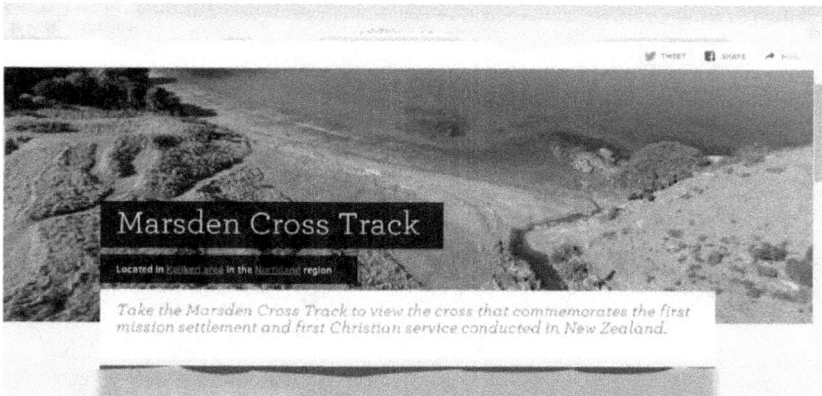

Marsden Cross Track

Located in Kerikeri area in the Northland region

Take the Marsden Cross Track to view the cross that commemorates the first mission settlement and first Christian service conducted in New Zealand.

The Marsden Cross Track – the cross that commemorates the first mission settlement and first Christian service conducted in New Zealand

Celebrating the bicentennial of beginnings

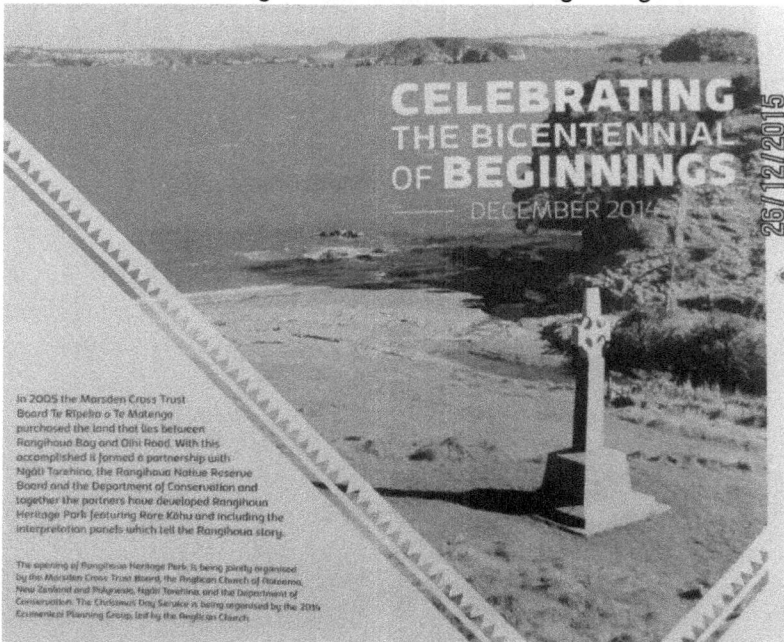

CELEBRATING THE BICENTENNIAL OF BEGINNINGS

DECEMBER 2014

26/12/2015

In 2005 the Marsden Cross Trust Board Te Rīpeka o Te Matenga purchased the land that lies between Rangihoua Bay and Oihi Road. With this accomplished it formed a partnership with Ngāti Torehina, the Rangihoua Native Reserve Board and the Department of Conservation and together the partners have developed Rangihoua Heritage Park featuring Rore Kāhu and including the interpretation panels which tell the Rangihoua story.

The opening of Rangihoua Heritage Park is being jointly organised by the Marsden Cross Trust Board, the Anglican Church of Aotearoa, New Zealand and Polynesia, Ngāti Torehina, and the Department of Conservation. The Christmas Day Service is being organised by the 2014 Ecumenical Planning Group, led by the Anglican Church.

The Marsden Cross situated a short distance from the shore

Brendan Jelley exploring the Marsden Cross surrounds

On Christmas Day 1814 the first Christian Service in N.Z. was held on this spot by the Rev Samuel Marsden.

1 – The Kendall house is next to the new school. Jane, Kendall's wife, recently gave birth to a son, rumoured to be fathered by Jane Kendal's servant, Richard Stockwell. 2 – The Mission School. William Hall is the Teacher to some 30 pupils, ranging in age from 7 to 20 year

Documented noticeboards at the Marsden Cross

Setting the scene – The Kendall's House and the School. The noticeboards are very detailed and informative

In memory of the Rangihoua Mission 1814 – 1854 and those buried here: -

John King
Hannah
Thomas Holloway
Samuel Leigh

Bus-type shelter with information board

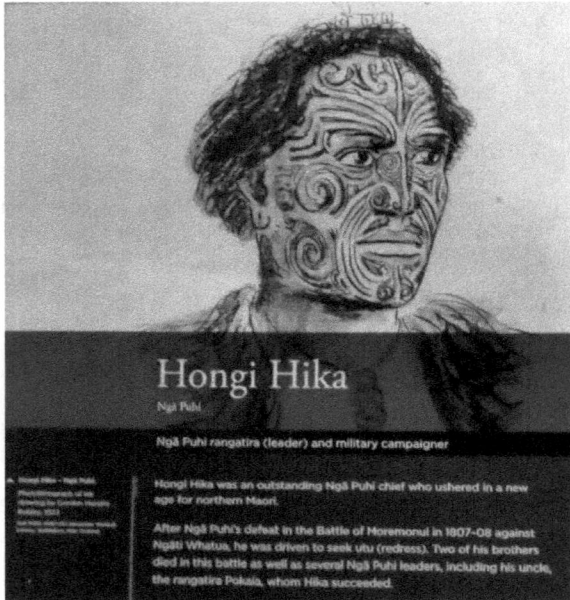

Hongi Hika

James and Charlotte Kemp – occupied and enlarged the Kerikeri house.

Kemp House – oldest building in New Zealand

Kerikeri Mission Station

Kemp House
1821

Kerikeri Mission Station – The Kemp House 1821

Shungee's Grant of Land at Keddee Keddee

NOVEMBER 4TH, 1819

Rec⁴ June 24/20   Com⁶ July 4/20

TO ALL TO WHOM THESE PRESENTS SHALL COME, GREETING. KNOW YE that I SHUNGHEE HEEKA Chief of the District of Ta Keddee Keddee at the Bay of Islands in the Island of New Zealand In consideration of Forty-eight Falling Axes to me faithfully paid and delivered by The Reverend SAMUEL MARSDEN Clerke for and on behalf of the Church of England Missionary Society HAVE GIVEN and GRANTED and of my free will and accord by these Presents Do give and grant to the Directors of the said Church of England Missionary Society and their successors for ever ALL that and those that Parcel of Land now called Pookay Kohay Ta Weedingha Tou etc. situate and lying in the District of Ta Keddee Keddee, and now known by the name of the Society's Plains containing thirteen thousand acres more or less, bounded on the South East by the District of the Chiefs Ta Morengha and Whytaroro, on the South West by the woods Weedingha Tou, Kyketayha Roa and Maungha Paray Dooa and on the North West and North East by the Road from Ta Too Honay to Ta Keddee Keddee With all the Timbers Minerals Waters Rights and Appurtenances to the same belonging To HOLD to the Directors of the said Church of England Missionary Society and their successors for ever IN FAITH AND TESTIMONY whereof I the said SHUNGHEE HEEKA have to these presents set and subscribed my seal at Ranghee Hou in the Island of New Zealand the fourth day of November in the year of Christ One thousand eight hundred and nineteen.

Sealed and Delivered in Presence of

JOHN BUTLER.
THOMAS KENDALL.

	The	
Signature of Rawha	Signature of	Shunghee
a chief and relation of Shunghee		Heeka

Shunghee Heeka	...	Hongi Hika.
Ta Keddee Keddee	...	Te Kerikeri (the Te is not usual)
Pookay Kohay	...	Puke Kowhai
Ta Weedingha Tou	...	Te Whiringatau
Ta Morengha	...	Te Morenga
Whytaroro	...	Waiteroro
Kyketayha Roa	...	Kahikatea Roa
Maungha Paray Dooa	...	Maunga Parerua
Ta Too Honay	...	Te Tuhonae
Ranghee Hou	...	Rangihoua
Rawha	...	Rewha
Rec⁴.	...	Received by the Secretary of the Church Missionary Society
Com⁶.	...	Placed before the Committee of the Church Missionary Society

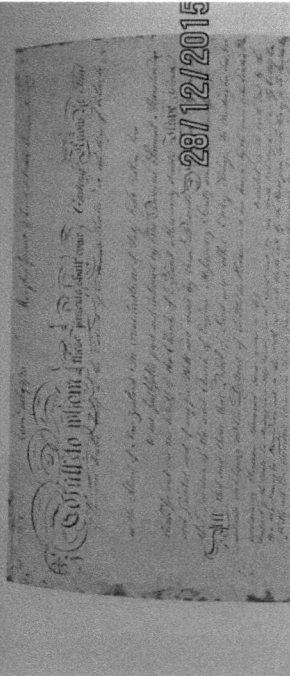

" Signatures to the grant :

THOS. KENDALL.

J. L. NICHOLAS. " ‡

SIGNATURES OF TE URI-O-KANAE AND MAORI N°"RUDA

Signed by Thomas Kendall and Maori 'Ahoodee O Gunna (Te Uri-o-Kanae) and his witness, for the grant of land at Kerikeri of 13,000 acres

Thomas Kendall

Location found - at last. First Christian 'church' service held 201 years ago (Christmas day 1814)

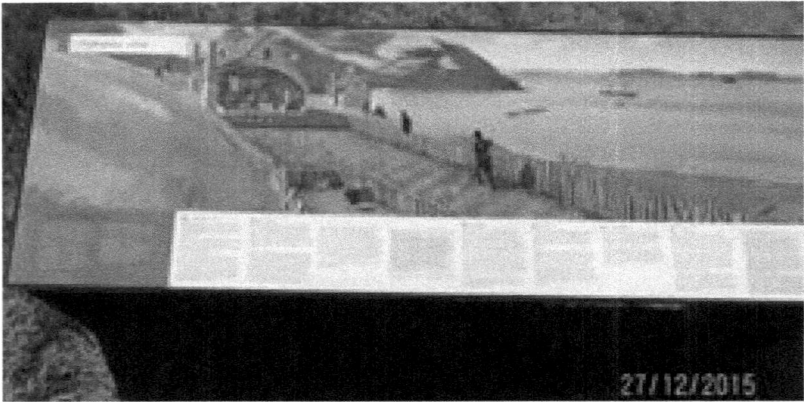

*Marsden's journeys in and around New Zealand - - He saw
more places that I have - and he did not have cars / roadways
200 years ago!!*

Second Journey = blue 1819

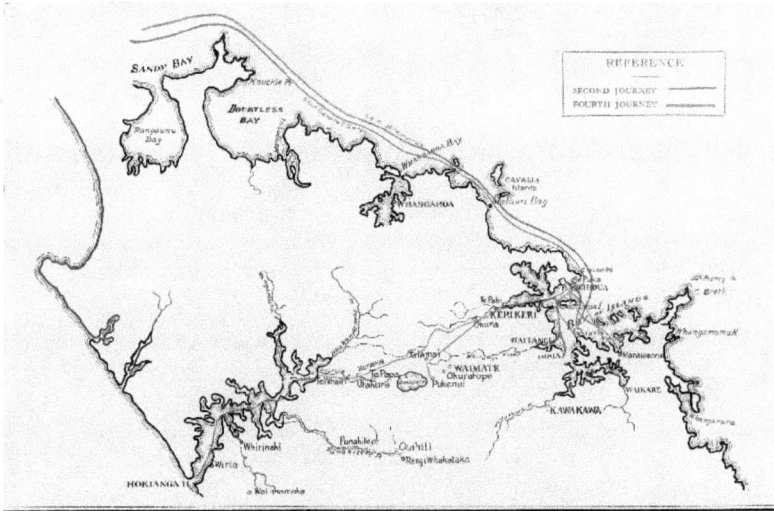

THE BAY OF ISLANDS AND HOKIANGA RIVER. To illustrate Marsden's journeys of 1819 and 1823

The Bay of Islands and the Hokianga River

Model of the Active at the entrance to the Waitangi Museum

The Brig Active

Bringing the missionary settlers to New Zealand

On 22nd December 1814, the brig Active, under the command of Captain Thomas Hansen, anchored in Rangihoua Bay, in the northern Bay of Islands. On board was Revd Samuel Marsden who had come to establish a missionary settlement next to the pā of his friend, the Māori chief, Ruatara.

There were three missionary families; those of John King, William Hall, and Thomas Kendall. Accompanying the missionaries was Thomas Hansen, the son of Captain Hansen and brother in law of John King.

The Active was a veritable 'Noah's Ark'. On board were horses, cattle, pigs, sheep, hens, fruit trees and seeds for crops, as Marsden intended that the mission station would be self-sufficient.

While William Hall and Thomas Kendall were destined to depart in 1825, John and Hannah King, together with Thomas and Elizabeth Hansen remained in the Bay of Islands for the remainder of their lives. They were New Zealand's first permanent, European settlers.

The Active

Built:	1808 (in Calcutta, India)
Class:	Brig
Length:	23 metres
Beam:	6.5 metres
Displacement:	110 tons
Crew:	9
Owner:	Revd Samuel Marsden

The arrival of the missionaries in the Bay of Islands on 22nd December 1814

(This model of the Active is on long term loan from the Hansen Family)

The Active

The 'Active' model, displayed in the entrance to the new museum at Waitangi

The Kerikeri Stone Store heritage site

Inevitably, Marsden was much misunderstood in his generation and just as often misrepresented. In essence, he was simple-minded and honest, even to a fault. He was also open-handed, almost prodigal with his time and his money. If he apparently neglected to evangelise the Aborigines it was not from want of trying. He also looked with pity on the fallen and the lost; he often befriended convicts. He was extraordinarily generous towards those who disappointed him, or even those who hated him. As he was always ready to admit, he could make mistakes, from human weakness, or from lack of counsellors in times of trouble. If he had a serious fault, it was his predisposition to take offence.

His role in the gradual emergence of New Zealand is difficult to assess. Without him the conversion of Maori to Christianity might have been long delayed. Marsden also transformed the Maori economy and laid the foundations of New Zealand agriculture. It can be said, too, that he made a notable contribution to the debate which ended in the British annexation of New Zealand. In 1831 he urged Darling to put a stop to the growing trade in tattooed heads, and protested with great energy the participation of a British captain and crew in the abduction and torture of Tama-i-hara-nui of Ngai Tahu by Ngati Toa. He urged the dispatch of a naval vessel with due power to restrain such scandalous misbehaviour, and recommended the appointment of a British Resident with proper authority, to whom Maori could appeal for redress.

However, Marsden recognised, all this would hardly be enough. He was far from objecting to the occasional colonisation of thinly peopled or vacant districts, and opined that if 'a body of good men were to sit down as Colonists...it would prove a great blessing to the Island.' Whatever the case, it would be necessary for some power to take New Zealand under its protection if the anarchy that prevailed at Kororareka (Russell) were not to become universal. That that power was ultimately Great Britain was in large measure due to the apostolic labours of Samuel Marsden.

He introduced winegrowing to New Zealand with the planting of over 100 different varieties of vine in Kerikeri, Northland. He wrote "New Zealand promises to be very favourable to the vine

as far as I can judge at present of the nature of the soil and climate".

The following extracts are from Dr. Shortland's Journal, 1843:

Pompallier Mission

Bishop Jeanhore-Baptiste Francois Pompallier, Vicar Apostolic to Western Oceania, arrived in New Zealand at Hokianga on the west coast in 1838.

The mission station in Kororareka encompassed the area surrounding what is now known as Pompallier House, Russell. A printing press was imported, and, with other Catholic missionaries, Pompallier sponsored the printing of prayer booklets in Maori, some of the earliest Māori publications. A tannery was set up to produce leather with which the pamphlets and books were bound.

Pompallier was present at Waitangi on the day before and the morning of the signing of the Treaty of Waitangi, which was held across the bay from Kororareka, on 6 February 1840. Pompallier pushed for a guaranteed freedom of religion. Pompallier was worried the treaty would hamper his mission and had advised some Catholic Maori chiefs not to sign the treaty. Having secured the statement of religious freedom he did not stay, he left the gathering after the discussion and before the parties signed.

Bishop Pompallier

Pompallier's picture in the glass-in-lead window in the church of Lapaha, Tonga

The trees in this reserve are part of a gift of 200 trees from the churches of Paeroa in 2014 to mark 200 years since the first recorded Christian service in New Zealand on Christmas Day 1814 at Oihi Bay in the Bay of Islands.

Rina and I were present in Paeroa when this site was commemorated in 2014

Year 2015 marked the bicentenary of the CMS mission to New Zealand, beginning Christmas Day, 1814.

New Zealand Missions in Northlands

The story of the New Zealand mission is a story of friendship and trust overcoming mutual misunderstanding and fear. It is a very human story of Missionary and Maori forbearing one another; tolerating, cajoling and forgiving one another; challenging each other, even threatening each other, but also laughing together at, and with each other - thus creating the space for a far more remarkable story to take root in New Zealand soil: the story of Te Rongopai o Ihu Karaiti, the Gospel of Jesus Christ; Te Kaiwhakaora mō te iwi katoa, the Saviour for all people. In marking this bicentenary year and looking particularly at the circumstances of that first Church Service, there are three significant themes that I wish to highlight.

1. Firstly, that the mission was founded upon mutual hospitality;
2. secondly, that the mission was Gospel centred; and lastly
3. that the beginning of the mission was marked by celebration.

If you look carefully, one may even see Rina sitting in the blue Nissan at the end of the cycle track, that runs past this grove where some of the 200 trees have been planted by the churches of Paeroa

Mutual Hospitality

The NZ mission was the culmination of a 20-year dream for Samuel Marsden. As the senior chaplain to the penal colony in New South Wales, he had seen these Māori adventurers arriving at the docks of Port Jackson having jumped on board passing ships. He would collect them and take them further up the harbour to Parramatta where he hosted them on his farm. There, Māori could receive instruction in agriculture and its attendant industries. But they were also able to observe his way of life, and his manner of worship. It was in Parramatta that Māori first heard about the Christian Gospel. Marsden, for his part, could observe the qualities of his Māori guests. Marsden's conclusion was that, the natives of New Zealand are far advanced in civilization, and apparently prepared for receiving the knowledge of Christianity more than any savage nation I have seen. Their habits of industry are very strong and

70

their thirst for knowledge great. They only want the means. It was this assessment that lead to his trip to England in 1807 and formed the basis of his proposal to CMS to establish a mission in New Zealand. The mission was not to be imposed on Māori but to be established with the cooperation and patronage of local Māori Rangatira. It is here that Ruatara becomes so significant. Marsden had first met Ruatara as the travelling companion of Te Pahi, his uncle, on his visit to Sydney in 1805. Marsden again encountered Ruatara on his return trip from England in 1809 as a fellow passenger on board the Ann. At that time Ruatara was very ill and was nursed back to health by Marsden and the ship's surgeon. Ruatara's keen interest in agriculture and strict observance of the Sabbath, made him in Marsden's mind the ideal patron for the new Mission. Ruatara had glimpsed something of what was possible for his own people in the Bay of Islands. This was not an easy vision to sell. He had returned with wheat seed to plant, which he distributed to his friends. When it was sprouted and grown green and tall, his friends pulled it all up expecting to find the fruit at its root, as with Kumara or Ferns. Finding nothing, however, they discounted the experiment yet another of Ruatara's stories. All, that is expect Hongi Hika. Hongi brought his crop through to harvest. But people still could not believe that the resulting seeds could be turned into bread, and despite being able to borrow a pepper mill from a ship anchored in the bay, Ruatara was not able to provide a definitive demonstration.

Gospel Centred

The second significant theme is that the mission was Gospel centred. Though, the way some recent scholars speak, you would be forgiven for not knowing that the New Zealand mission had anything to do with religion. In their re-telling of the story, it was all about the establishment of the first school in New Zealand by Thomas Kendall. However, the story cannot be told without the Gospel at its heart. Ruatara, after the formal welcome, spent the rest of Christmas Eve preparing for the next day. It was all his own initiative: he knew that the next day was the Sabbath, the Rātapu. He enclosed 1/2 an acre of land with a fence, built a reader's desk and pulpit and covered them with black flax cloth. He even provided pews for the Pākehā—planks supported by upturned canoes. By these preparations Ruatara intended the gathering the next day to be a fully-fledged service of Christian worship, as he had experienced them at Parramatta. On Christmas morning, the Union Jack flew from the top of Rangihoua Pā to signal the day. When the missionary party arrived on shore they took their seats either side of the pulpit.

Ruatara's friendship with Marsden, however, was sufficiently strong for him to accept Marsden's invitation to make a return visit to Parramatta along with Hongi Hika and Korokoro, and consequently to accept Marsden's proposal of a missionary settlement in the Bay of Islands. Marsden returned with them to the Bay of Islands along with the three missionary families of Kendall, Hall and King. The three chiefs returned with a few gifts, including military uniforms given to them by Governor Lachlan Macquarie as a mark of his respect for their chiefly status. Korokoro was so impressed by the Governor that, in customary Māori fashion, he proposed a personal change of name to Governor Macquarie.

Their ship, the Active, arrived off Hohi Bay, beside Ruatara's Pā at Rangihoua just before Christmas Day, 1814. Hohi Bay being the local Māori name for what later became known as Oihi bay. As well as exchanging gifts, including presenting Ruatara's head-wife, Rahu, with a red gown and petticoat from Marsden's wife, Elizabeth, Marsden unloaded several cows and horses, causing a sensation amongst the locals. They had heard stories from Ruatara, as he attempted to explain to them a horse and carriage— 'It's a four-legged animal like a dog or pig,' said Ruatara, 'only big enough for a man to ride on its back. And these animals are used to pull 'land canoes'', he said, 'in which people ride.' Some had stuck their fingers in their ears and refused to listen, others attempted to mount some nearby pigs to ride them as Ruatara described, only to be thrown off into the dirt and for everyone to fall about laughing. Yet now, Ruatara was vindicated, as Marsden astonished everyone by mounting one of the horses and riding up and down the beach.

On Christmas Eve, Korokoro, or as he now wished to be called, Governor Macquarie, returned from the south side of the Bay with 200 of his warriors to provide a formal welcome party for the new settlers. They gathered the Europeans from their ship and made for the shore. Ruatara was ready with his men, though only one warrior could be seen prancing up and down the beach. After a stirring haka, Korokoro's warriors rush ashore chasing the lone toa off the beach only to be met by Ruatara's men descending upon them down the valley. A furious mock-fight ensued until all were exhausted.

John Nicholas, one of the observers, marvelled at Rahu, Ruatara's wife, in the thick of the fight, in her new red dress, banishing a large horse-pistol. With everyone's energy expended, the welcome concluded with haka and food. A fitting tribute to the new mission that was founded on the principles of friendship, trust, welcome and hospitality.

Surrounding them all were the local people of the Pā. The three chiefs, Ruatara, Hongi and Korokoro, were dressed in their regimentals, swords by their sides. The Service began with the old 100th. Based on Psalm 100, it is one of the oldest hymns in the English language (1561), written by a Scotsman in exile in Geneva. But a most appropriate hymn for the occasion, as it invites 'all people' to join with the 'angelic host' in joyful praise to God: The Father, the Son and the Holy Spirit. The Service was read—people standing or sitting as directed by Korokoro with a baton. Then Samuel Marsden rose to deliver his sermon. His text was Luke 2:10, 'Behold, I bring you good tidings of great joy.' What a great Gospel text! It concerns the 'good tidings', te rongo pai. What a great mission text! For the good tidings are for 'all people', te iwi katoa. Ever since James Belich's history, *Making Peoples*, it's been popular to claim that in fact no sermon was preached that day. It's not denied that Marsden rose to speak, but that Ruatara's words that followed were not at all a translation of what was said. They were more by way of a reassurance to Māori that their display of earnest attention would be amply rewarded by the riches of missionary trade.

It was Marsden's intention that he should preach a sermon, and Ruatara's intention (as his preparations demonstrated) that Māori would hear a sermon. So, despite the naysayers, there was a sermon that Christmas morning!

This was the Service that marked the beginning of Christian mission in New Zealand. This was the sermon preached at that Service—even if only a few could comprehend it. There was a sermon that Christmas morning! Secondly, and more importantly, James Belich makes the mistaken assumption that Marsden had little, if any, facility in te reo Māori. It is known that this was not the case. Marsden had been in contact with Māori from the beginning of his time in NSW, but undertook more intensive language study, with Ruatara as his tutor, during their 5-month return voyage from England five years before. At that stage, Marsden claimed that he could speak to Ruatara 'on any common subject and can make myself clearly understood.' He only wished that William Hall and John King had taken a similar advantage of the opportunity that was presented (Kendall and his family were to arrive in Sydney a little later). Marsden was fully cognisant of the importance to the mission of his own ability to speak the language and consequently was a motivated learner.

Thirdly, even if Marsden didn't utilise Māori during his sermon, he certainly had enough knowledge of the language to be aware of what Ruatara was saying by way of interpretation. So, to argue that Ruatara ignored Marsden's spiritual message and instead interposed his own more political agenda is not at all convincing. Besides which, it ignores the trust that had developed between Marsden and Ruatara over the five years of their friendship. Fourthly, as we will see a little later, Ngā Puhi oral tradition suggests that Māori did in fact appreciate the spiritual significance of what was occurring. It wasn't just about trade goods, even if Māori couldn't fully appreciate what Marsden was saying.

If, as we are rightly told, Māori of this period had an all-embracing spiritual worldview, how can it then be expected that Māori received the missionaries on such secular terms? No, Ngā Puhi accounts of that day indicate that Māori paid great attention to the spiritual significance of what was coming among them.

Two Questions arise? So, did Marsden preach in Māori? And what do we know of the sermon's message? Firstly, did Marsden preach in Māori? David Pettett, an Australian scholar undertaking doctoral research on Marsden's sermons, makes the case that yes, in fact, he did. And the case for saying so is much stronger than you might think! We have three eyewitness accounts of what happened: John Nicholas (Marsden's companion on the trip who kept a detailed journal that he later published); John King (one of the three settler missionaries who wrote a letter a few weeks later), and Marsden himself.

None of these sources rule out the possibility that Marsden spoke in Māori and at various points provide us with positive indications that he did. For instance, we learn from Marsden's journal that he was interrupted during the sermon by Maori speaking to Ruatara and saying, (in Marsden's words) 'they could not understand what I meant.' It may have been due to his accent, or his grammar, or his subject matter, but it is an altogether odd interjection to make if Marsden was speaking in English, a language that Māori were not expected to understand at all. Over the years, the various missionaries were generally able to quickly pick up a level of 'trade' Māori sufficient for day-to-day co-existence, usually within the first year after their arrival. So, there is no difficulty in maintaining that Marsden, with a 10-20-year exposure to the language, had at least this level of proficiency, if not far more. He was probably among the best European speakers of te reo Māori in the colony at the time. It was the later challenge of translating the scriptures that really tested the missionaries' facility with the language. For Marsden to preach at least part of his sermon in Māori would have been difficult, but not impossible. Turning to our second question, what do we know of the sermon's content? There are three extant sermons by Marsden on this verse, but unfortunately none of them appear to be the one preached on this occasion. Most probably, Marsden spoke extemporarily and had few if any notes. However, David Pettett has assembled a reconstruction of the sermon in outline, based on the three known manuscripts. If nothing else, it highlights the strongly expositional nature of Marsden's preaching. Comparing themes from each of the sermons, he thinks Marsden could have made any, or all, of the following eight points:

1. The birth of Christ is the most important event the world has ever seen.

2. It is good tidings of great joy for all people.

3. This event has been long and anxiously expected by the faithful.

4. Those who are awaiting a temporal messiah will be disappointed because this Messiah brings spiritual blessings.

5. This event has been announced with great rejoicing by the angels of heaven who have declared a Saviour for mankind.

6. This Messiah was not born in a palace, but a stable, making him accessible to all people.

7. This is the superior Saviour because he defeats the Evil One and saves from Hell.

8. Now is the time to follow this Saviour because you may not be alive next Christmas season.

What these eight points demonstrate, was that Marsden was not setting up a school, nor was he advocating some simple equation that civilisation would lead to Christianisation. What is clear is that Marsden intended for the New Zealand mission to be firmly centred on the Gospel, and for education and the 'arts' of civilisation to go together with seeking the conversion of Māori to Christ. The New Zealand mission was founded on mutual hospitality and it was Gospel-centred. The last significant theme that I would like to highlight is that the beginning of the mission was marked by celebration.

Celebration

Once the Service was finished, the Europeans proceeded out of the enclosure only to be startled by a haka from the 400 warriors present. Although for the Europeans it was a rather surprising, though welcome, end to the Service, it was a perfectly fitting response for Māori to make, given what had occurred over the previous three days. It was the culmination of their reception for this rather 'strange tribe' of missionaries who had come into their midst.

Patricia Bawden in her book, *The Years Before Waitangi*, makes mention of a Ngā Puhi tradition concerning the words to that haka passed on to her by Sir James Henare. More recently, the Anglican bishop Te Kitohi Pikaahu, the bishop responsible for the Hui Amorangi of Te Tai Tokerau (which extends over the area of Northland for Tikanga Māori) has corroborated this tradition.

Namely, that the words of the haka performed that day referred to the coming of the Pipiwhararauroa, the shining cuckoo, a migratory bird whose piercing cry announces the arrival of spring. Songs were (and are) very important to Māori and carried great significance. The sharing of a song was sufficient to forge new alliances or call allies together for war. So, the oral tradition concerning the words of this haka confirms that Māori were aware of the welcome they were extending to Marsden and the missionaries. But more importantly, it was a haka that sounded a true note of celebration, heralding the dawn of a new partnership between Māori and Pākehā established upon the Gospel of Jesus Christ.

When Marsden had returned to the *Active*, he wrote these words in his diary: "*In the above manner, the Gospel has been introduced into New Zealand, and I fervently pray that the glory of it may never depart from its inhabitants till time shall be no more*". (extracted from the Internet).

Marsden's' Legacy

Samuel Marsden founded the following CMS Mission Stations in New Zealand: -

- Tepuna – John King – Dec 1814
- Whangaroa – James Kemp – Aug 1819
- Kerikeri – James Shepherd – Feb 1820
- Paihia – Rev. Henry Williams – Aug 1923
- Waimate – Clarke / Davis / Williams – Apr 1824
- Mangpouri – James Hamlin – Mar 1826
- Matamata – Rev Alfred Brown – Nov 1929
- Rotorua – Thomas Chapman – Jul 1830
- Puriri – James Preece – Dec 1830
- Kaitaia – Joseph Matthews – Mar 1832
- Kerikeri – John Edmonds (Stonemason) – Feb 1834
- Tauranga – Philip Hansen King – Feb 1834

A visit to the model mission station at Waimate is a real eye-opener, to appreciate the very deep spoor that Marsden tread.

The mission station has already been visited twice and another is needed to satisfy curiosity.

Marsden Cove

The location of New Zealand's largest oil refinery is situated across the estuary from Whangarei.

Marsden Bay – where the oil refinery is located

Marsden Bay

The Marsden Estate – Kerikeri. Situated on the Kerikeri airport road.

The owner, kindly allowed me to catch sight of his valuable, two-volume books on Samuel Marsden. Marsden did introduce vine growing in the Kerikeri district.

Marsden Builders – Kopu / Thames

Marsden Builders in Kopu, Thames, have not been checked out; their eye-catching signboard was noted during one of our frequent trips to the Coromandel Peninsular.

Marsden Builders Ltd
25 State Hwy 26, KOPU, THAMES
Marshall Hutt : Ph. 0274 944 233

LETTERS
AND
JOURNALS
OF
SAMUEL
MARSDEN

MARSDEN
LIEUTENANT

PINOTAGE

The winery takes its name from the Reverend Samuel Marsden who planted New Zealand's first grape vines in the Bay Of Islands. Situated in one of New Zealand's warmest regions Marsden Estate is dedicated to the production of quality wines.

Pinotage: The exceptional 2014 summer has produced this rich, ripe Pinotage. Picked at over 25 brix the nose hints of raspberries and spice. The palate is generous savoury and warm with enveloping lush tannins and good depth. Cellar 2-8 years.

MARSDEN
BAY OF ISLANDS

Pinotage

2014

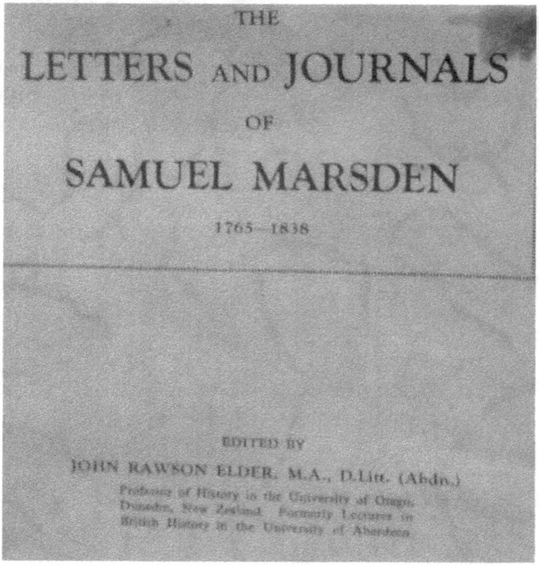

THE

LETTERS AND JOURNALS

OF

SAMUEL MARSDEN

1765—1838

EDITED BY

JOHN RAWSON ELDER, M.A., D.Litt. (Abdn.)

Professor of History in the University of Otago,
Dunedin, New Zealand. Formerly Lecturer in
British History in the University of Aberdeen

This copy was obtained by the Paeroa Library. It is a very rare, signed copy by the author, John Elder.

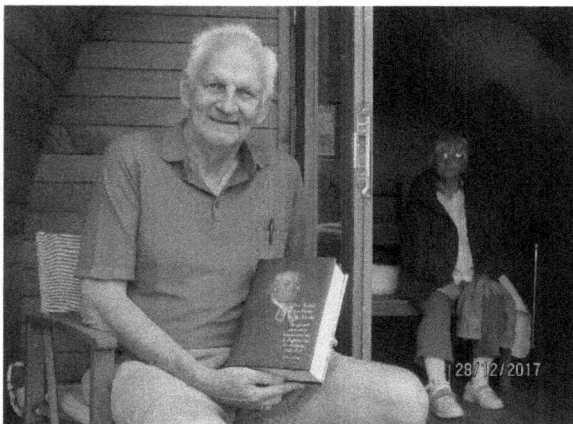

The author with a copy of Andrew Sharp's 2016 "The World, the Flesh & the Devil", who delved into the mind of Samuel Marsden – a man of formidable energy.

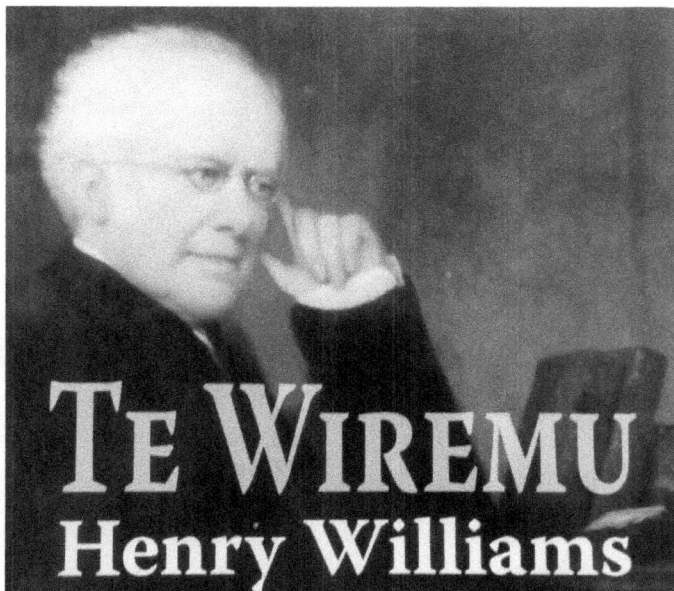

Caroline Fitzgerald's book about her great-great-grandfather needs to be on every New Zealander's bookshelf.

Bibliography

Patricia Bawden, *The Years Before Waitangi*

Judith Binney *Te Kerikeri 1770 – 1850*, Bridget Williams Books, 2007

Colville Historical Committee *In the Shadows of Moehau* 1990

John Rawson Elder, *The Letters and Journals of Samuel Marsden*, Otago University, 1932

John Rawson Elder, *The Letters and Journals of Samuel Marsden 1765 - 1838*

Caroline Fitzgerald *Te Wiremu Henry Williams,* Huia Publishers, 2011

Frontier of Dreams, the Story of New Zealand, TVNZ, Bronwyn Dalley and Gavin McLean, 2005

Angela Middleton, *Pewhairangi Bay of Islands Missions and Maori 1814 to 1845*, Otago Press, 2014

J. C. Beaglehole; "*Exploration of the Pacific*" -

Angela Middleton *Pewhairangi Bay of Islands Missions and Maori 1814 to 1845*, Otago 2014

Andrew Sharp *The World, the Flesh & the Devil,* Auckland University Press, 2016

The *New Zealand Railways Magazine*, Volume 15, Issue 2 (May 1, 1940.)

G. S. Parsonson and was first published in the *Dictionary of New Zealand Biography* Volume 1, 1990

Pompallier Mission, NZ Historic Places Trust – ouhere Taonga, 2007

Richard Wolfe *Hell-hole of the Pacific*, Penguin Books, 2005

Index

86

87

www.ingramcontent.com/pod-product-compliance
Lightning Source LLC
Chambersburg PA
CBHW071107090426
42737CB00013B/2515